Caribbean Masala

CARIBBEAN
STUDIES
SERIES

Anton L. Allahar and Natasha Barnes
Series Editors

Caribbean Masala

Masala
Indian Identity in
Guyana and Trinidad

DAVE RAMSARAN AND LINDEN F. LEWIS

University Press of Mississippi / Jackson

www.upress.state.ms.us

The University Press of Mississippi is a member of
the Association of University Presses.

First printing 2018

∞

Library of Congress Cataloging-in-Publication Data

Names: Ramsaran, Dave, author. | Lewis, Linden, 1953– author.
Title: Caribbean masala : Indian identity in Guyana and Trinidad / Dave
Ramsaran and Linden F. Lewis.
Description: Jackson : University Press of Mississippi, [2018] | Series:
Caribbean studies series | Includes bibliographical references and index.
| Identifiers: LCCN 2017058597 (print) | LCCN 2018000677 (ebook) | ISBN
9781496818058 (epub single) | ISBN 9781496818065 (epub institutional) |
ISBN 9781496818072 (pdf single) | ISBN 9781496818089 (pdf institutional)
| ISBN 9781496818041 (cloth : alk. paper)
Subjects: LCSH: Group identity—Caribbean Area. | East Indians—Trinidad and
Tobago—Trinidad—History. | East Indians—Guyana—History.
Classification: LCC F2191.E27 (ebook) | LCC F2191.E27 R37 2018 (print) | DDC
972.9/004914—dc23
LC record available at https://lccn.loc.gov/2017058597

British Library Cataloging-in-Publication Data available

Contents

Acknowledgments

We would like to thank all those people who, in one way or another, have assisted us in bringing this manuscript to fruition. Among them are all the participants in our focus groups, the men in our in-depth interviews, and those from our chance conversations in Guyana and Trinidad. Their willingness to participate in our research is greatly appreciated. We would also like to acknowledge the editorial work done on an early draft of this manuscript by Molly Clay. In addition to editing the volume, Molly pushed us to achieve greater clarity in our arguments, and she raised many interesting questions about our work. We very much appreciate the photographic contributions of Sherry Dubarry, some of whose pictures were used in this book. Thanks also to Andrea de Silva for her permission to reprint her photograph of Samdaye Sonny. Lastly, we would like to thank the two reviewers of this book for their insightful queries and helpful comments on our work.

Caribbean Masala

Introduction

"Masala" is a Hindi word that refers to mixed spices. At one level, the word is used in the title of this book as a metaphor not only for the Indo-Caribbean communities of Trinidad and Guyana[1] but also for the broader Caribbean region. The Caribbean area includes people of African, Indian, Portuguese, Chinese, Syrian, and Lebanese descent, none of whom is indigenous to the region. Different historical and social forces brought these disparate groups of people to the Caribbean, in some cases under extremely oppressive and alienating circumstances. Some came to the region forcibly, as in the case of people of African descent. Others, although coming voluntarily (for the most part), as was the case of most people of Indian descent, later found their conditions of service not far removed from the slavery of their African predecessors. Others such as the Portuguese and Chinese, who also arrived under the system of indenture, found that prejudices and stereotypes tended to marginalize them, placing them at odds with the more dominant African and Indian populations of the region. Irrespective of how they entered the region, these various groups all had to adapt and make accommodations in this new environment. Those native to the area, the Arawaks, Caribs, and Tainos, were essentially decimated by Christopher Columbus and his invading interlopers. In the context of Guyana, however, the indigenous population has a long, enduring history, perhaps going back more than twelve thousand years. Today, there are nine existing indigenous groups in Guyana accounting for 7 percent of the population.

Caribbean Masala, then, focuses on the ambivalent processes of mixing, assimilating, and adapting on one level, while trying desperately to hold onto that which marks a group of people as distinct, different, and somewhat separate. The lived experience of the Indian community in Guyana and Trinidad in some ways represents a cultural contradiction of belonging and nonbelonging—of being a part of all that is the Caribbean yet not wanting to belong so completely as to be overwhelmed by the dominance of the African presence in the Caribbean, which confronts them on all levels.

In this work, we settle on the terms "Indian," "Indian descent," and "Indo-Trinidadian" or "Indo-Guyanese." We have shied away from the term "East Indian," which was used largely because of Columbus's mistaken belief that he had reached the East when in fact he had arrived in the Caribbean, and so the term was based on a misconception. In addition, the term "East Indian" tends to be used as a way to distinguish people of Indian descent from those who are directly from the subcontinent. Indians from India are not only seen as more authentic genealogically than their Caribbean descendants, but are also viewed as culturally different from the Indo-Caribbean people of Guyana and Trinidad. We are, however, fully cognizant that the use of the term "Indian" does not resolve all definitional problems, as the writer V. S. Naipaul (2003, 39) reminds us: "To be an Indian from Trinidad is to be unlikely. It is, in addition to everything else, to be the embodiment of an old verbal ambiguity. For this word 'Indian' has been abused as no other word in the language; almost every time it is used it has to be qualified." Of course, there are somewhat less grave social consequences, which are captured in an exchange between Naipaul and a fellow traveler waiting for a flight from London to Paris:

> "You are coming from—?"
>
> I had met enough Indians from India to know that this was less a serious inquiry than a greeting, in a distant land, from one Indian to another.
>
> "Trinidad," I said. "In the West Indies. And you?"

He ignored my question. "But you look Indian."

"I am."

"Red Indian?" He suppressed a nervous little giggle.

"East Indian. From the West Indies."

He looked offended and wandered off to the bookstall. From this distance he eyed me assessingly. In the end curiosity overcame misgiving. He sat next to me on the bus to the airport. He sat next to me in the plane. (2003, 35)

It should be noted at this point that the numbers of people of Indian descent in Guyana and Trinidad are significant—in fact, Indians outnumber all other groups in both countries, with 39.9 percent and 35.4 percent, respectively—the only other country where Indians exist in such significant numbers being Suriname (37 percent). In other parts of the Caribbean, Indians are not as demographically strong. In places such as Martinique (10 percent), Saint Lucia (2.2 percent), Saint Kitts and Nevis (1.9 percent), and Grenada (0.4 percent), people of Indian descent are often so absorbed into the more dominant African culture, and through marriage to non-Indians, that the issue of an Indo-Caribbean sense of heritage figures only peripherally in national discourses on identity. This observation prompted V. S. Naipaul to observe:

Growing up in multiracial Trinidad as a member of the Indian community, people brought over in the late nineteenth and early twentieth centuries to work the land, I always knew how important it was not to fall into nonentity. In 1961, when I was traveling in the Caribbean for my first travel book, I remember my shock, my feeling of taint and spiritual annihilation, when I saw some of the Indians of Martinique, and began to understand that they had been swamped by Martinique, that I had no means of sharing the world view of these people whose history at some stage had been like mine, but who now, racially and in other ways, had become something other. (1989, 33)

Amartya Sen describes this cultural erosion as "identity disregard"—a "form of ignoring, or neglecting altogether, the influence of any sense of identity with others, on what we value and how we behave" (2006, 20). While certain Indian rituals and customs persist in parts of the Caribbean, they do not always constitute a central or dominant part of the identity of those who perform them. Naipaul's comments are a reflection of the time and perhaps his own narrow reading of people of Indian descent in Martinique. There is a greater interest in matters of identity and heritage in the contemporary French Caribbean than there was when Naipaul was writing about the region.

Sen's observation is similarly perhaps too strong an assessment of the situation in some parts of the Caribbean, but it points to the fact that, apart from Guyana, Trinidad, and Suriname, ethnic identity in the region does not constitute significant levels of contestation and conflict. We argue, therefore, that in Guyana and Trinidad these matters are the result of demographic constituency and social and political influence. Kumar Mahabir (2009, 79) notes that there are similar issues of cultural salience and identity in Saint Vincent; however, Indians there form distinct communities and tend to marry within their own community.

CREOLIZATION AND THE FRAMING OF THE INDIAN COMMUNITY

Our focus in this book will revolve around the theoretical perspective of creolization, which is in keeping with the notion of mixing, assimilating, and adapting but which also allows us to come to terms with the fact that these are two groups of people, in Trinidad and Guyana, whose origin is elsewhere, in the Indian subcontinent, but who have had to carve out a space for themselves in lands that are not only foreign but at times even hostile to them. George Lamming's point about the power of the creolization process to affect those who are subjected to it is well taken here:

> Time and the political economy of the landscape in the form of the plantation allowed no one to be exempt from the inexorable process of creolization. There are those who claim European ancestry,

but who were made, shaped, and seeded by the cultural forces of the archipelago, and whose interaction with others have [sic] made them a distinct breed from the stock from whom they have descended. (2009, 59)

Kusha Haraksingh's observation addresses a different angle of the creolization process in that it brilliantly captures the extent to which Indians were faced with the choice of returning to India or settling in their adopted homes. In the end, many of them made the decision to stay—some because economic constraints forced them to remain, others because they had already begun to establish roots in the Caribbean, and yet others because they anticipated that a return to their native land may not have been as hospitable as imagined. These options are remarkably captured in the following passage:

The decision to stay was often coupled with a residential move away from plantations to "free" villages, which itself often involved the acquisition of title to property. This served as a major platform for belonging, an urge that soon became more evident in efforts to redesign the landscape. Thus, the trees which were planted around emergent homesteads, including religious vegetation, constituted a statement about belonging; so too did the temples and mosques which began to dot the landscape. And the rearing of animals which could not be abandoned; and the construction of ponds and tanks; and the diversion of watercourses; and the clearing of the lands. When all of this is put together it is hard to resist the conclusion that Indians had begun to think of Trinidad as their home long before general opinion in the country had awakened to that as a possibility. (Haraksingh 1999, 40)

Haraksingh's comments above hold equally true for Indians in Guyana as well.

The process of mixing, however, is brought into sharp relief by Lamming's observation about the nature of the inescapable impact of social reproduction in the Caribbean:

Moreover, the relations of intimacy, voluntary or otherwise, which diagnosed plantation society in the Caribbean did not allow for any reliable claim to any form of ancestral purity. Creole is the name of their anatomy. The sons and daughters of Indian indentured labor arriving in the third decade of the 19th century may argue a stronger case for ancestral heritage than their African predecessors, but this proximity in time to the ancestral homeland does not erase or obscure their sense of belonging to the creolized world of Trinidad or Guyana. (2009, 59–60)

The actions of establishing roots in the Caribbean described by Haraksingh are also consistent with the concept of "coolitude" articulated by Khal Torabully and cited by Smita Tripathi (2009, 161): namely, that Indian identity is not merely concerned with nostalgia for an ancestral homeland but is also rooted in "relationships engendered by the indenture-ship system itself." As mentioned earlier, however, this rootedness indexes both a sense of belonging and a fear that belonging implies some form of cultural pollution, or acculturation, if not total assimilation. It is a tension that has to be wrestled with constantly by Indians in Guyana and Trinidad. The tension between people of African and Indian descent sometimes manifests itself in the folklore of racial identity as brilliantly captured by Rahul Bhattacharya's novel, *The Sly Company of People Who Care*:

Take the one [story] recounted to me at the bar in the cricket club by a lawyer. The case was a lady he'd once badgered so hard in the witness box that she fainted. A year after the event she knocked on his door. "Thick Indian girl, country manners, powder on chest." He was not good with faces, but he remembered her on account of the fainting. She wanted to retain him. She had been accused of killing her own baby. Everybody suspected that the child was by a black man. Certainly her behavior was odd. She would shave the child's head every week, so nobody got to see its hair. And when the child died she didn't report it, she buried it. She claimed he choked on his vomit. (2011, 5)

Although anecdotal, the above description is typical of a scenario that is embedded into the folklore of racial identity, in which somatic features such as hair texture, and shape and size of noses and lips, index not just racial categories but racial purity and authenticity. The passage indicates that straight or curly hair reveals much about racial belonging and nonbelonging. One has to go to great lengths to establish racial bona fides. Bhattacharya is once again humorous but perceptively insightful in this regard:

> I felt he looked it and asked him if he was mixed: it was polite conversation in Guyana. I hurt him. "Pure, man," he said defensively. "Pure all the way." He took off his cap, ran his hand over his very short hair, buzzed down on the scalp. He pulled the strands up to their exerted millimetres, inviting me to touch. "Watch man, straight. It straight."
> (2011, 80)

Beyond the impact of the cultural landscape of Guyana and Trinidad on people of Indian descent in the Caribbean is their own influence on the societies in which they live. What may have started out as essentially Indian—whether Hindu or Muslim—traditions and rituals have become nationalized and celebrated by many people in Guyana and Trinidad who are not of Indian descent. The Muslim celebration of the festival of Hosein (or Hosay), and the holiday of Eid al-Fitr marking the end of the fasting of Ramadan, are not confined to the Indian Muslim community in Trinidad; they are truly nationally observed rituals. All celebrate Diwali, the Hindu festival of lights, perhaps more so in Trinidad than in Guyana. Phagwah (Holi) is another Hindu celebration of good over evil that is generally recognized nationally in both Guyana and Trinidad and not restricted to participation by Indians. We will return to the Phagwah celebration later. Indian Arrival Day is also a celebrated holiday in Guyana and Trinidad, and, as with the others mentioned here, is recognized as a national holiday or observed generally in both countries. Accompanying the process of creolization, then, is a corresponding dynamic process of the Indian impact on the societies of Guyana and Trinidad.

We should be mindful, however, of homogenizing the creolizing experience of the Indian communities in the two countries. As Anton Allahar and Tunku Varadarajan note, "the process of creolisation has

touched these two communities in very different ways, and has produced a series of differential creolisations" (1994). These authors go on
to make a nuanced point about the perception of difference between
Trinidadian and Guyanese Indians:

> In Trinidad creole culture has penetrated the East Indian community
> far more deeply than in Guyana. This is due in part to two factors: (a)
> the East Indians in Guyana enjoy a greater numerical majority than
> their Trinidadian counterparts, and are able to use that majority to
> insulate themselves, if only temporarily, against the tide of creolisa-
> tion, and (b) Guyana is not as economically developed as Trinidad
> and the predominantly rurally-based Indo-Guyanese in particular
> are less subject to the forces of urbanization, industrialization and
> secularization that have proved so decisive in eroding traditional
> cultures and conditioning the rise of new, modern creole cultures.
> (1994, 123–24)

Although there is some merit to the above observation, we differ
from the authors for the following reasons. First, we believe that their
observation is only partially true. While there are differences between
Indo-Trinidadians and Indo-Guyanese, we are more persuaded by the
historical evidence indicating that the Indo-Guyanese community
became polarized from other groups in Guyana and formed separate,
though not entirely closed, communities. This polarization was largely
due to efforts of specifically racialized political parties, which were
opposed to each other. Subsequently, a strategy of political mobilization developed on the basis of race. Although similar dynamics may
exist in Trinidad somewhat below the surface, tensions rarely boil over
into full-blown racial conflict, rioting, and murder, as have occurred
repeatedly in Guyana since the 1960s. We would argue that there are
certainly differences in the experience of creolization between the
Indian communities in the two countries but that these differences
emanate from the specific racial formation of Guyana and the political
exploitation of racial difference, more so than any notion of lack of
urbanization or secularization among the Indo-Guyanese.

Second, because the Indo-Guyanese have mostly lived and worked in the rural areas of Guyana, in places such as Annandale and Berbice, and near sugar and rice plantations, one could argue that Indians have had and still have a rural base centered around agriculture. Nonetheless, Indians have for some time now been integrated into Guyanese society, and it would be inaccurate to claim that they have not been urbanized, industrialized, or secularized. Greater access to education, among other factors, has integrated Indians into the teaching profession, the civil service, the business community, and the international organizations operating in Guyana. Furthermore, this process of urbanization has intensified since 1992 with the return to power of the People's Progressive Party (PPP) under President Cheddi Jagan, eventually followed by Bharrat Jagdeo. It would be misleading to describe the Indo-Guyanese as merely rural residents, untouched by notions of modernity.

Third, despite the differences that exist between the Indo-Guyanese and Indo-Trinidadians, we have observed that despite being in different countries, there have always been friendly relations between the two racial groups and that intermarriage between them is not uncommon. Particularly since 1992, with the return of the PPP to office in Guyana, there have been increasing economic and political ties between political parties from the respective countries, which are predominantly Indian identified. In the first instance, the former prime minister of Trinidad and Tobago, Basdeo Panday, established close links with Cheddi Jagan of Guyana. When these leaders had left office, the cooperative relationship solidified between President Bharrat Jagdeo and Prime Minister Kamla Persad-Bissessar of Trinidad. We have no reason to doubt that this collaboration in political and economic terms continued between the Persad-Bissessar government and Jagdeo's successor in Guyana, Donald Ramotar. It is still too early to tell if the ascendancy of A Partnership for National Unity/Alliance for Change (APNU/AFC) in Guyana, a coalition of African and Indian politicians that came to power in May 2015, would set a different course with the new Trinidadian government led by Keith Rowley, whose People's National Movement is a largely African-based party.

Such linkages are destined to flatten out the differences between these two groups who share the same ancestral background.

We argue, then, that despite its shortcomings, the creole model provides us with the most appropriate theoretical framework for understanding the Indian communities in Guyana and Trinidad. The "Creole Society" model popularized by social historian Kamau Brathwaite attempts to account for Caribbean social processes by looking at the influences of the major cultural groups that inhabit the region. This approach sees Caribbean society as evolving through mutual adjustments and reciprocal interactions within and among the major cultural sectors. Two processes, acculturation and interculturation, are at work in this model. The former involves the yoking and forced absorption of one culture by another in a one-way direction. This process accounts for the dominance of European culture in some areas of the Caribbean experience. The latter is more of an osmotic process that involves a two-way exchange in particular historical circumstances. As such, slaves were acculturated into a "fixed superiority/inferiority relationship" and forced to adopt white norms (Reddock 1998, 416). Over time, whites also succumbed in functionally different ways to the powerful influences of the creolizing impetus of African cultural patterns through the process of interculturation: "This creole society, however is not culturally homogenous, one can speak of a continuum related to class, color and ethnicity with predominantly Euro-creole forms forming the higher, more acceptable side of the continuum and Afro-creole forms . . . at the lower end of acceptability" (Reddock 1998, 417).

Two schools of thought have attempted to incorporate Indo-Trinidadian culture into this "Creole Society" model, and some suggest that Indo-Trinidadian culture remains separate and distinct. Another view is that, over time, the Indo-Trinidadian community has been assimilated into the dominant "Creole/Euro-Christian culture" (Reddock 1998, 418). Rhoda Reddock suggests a view we share, which is that both approaches are essentially correct. Indo-Trinidadians are being absorbed into the mainstream particularly as the process of globalization envelops society, while, simultaneously, they have also re-created creolized forms and spaces of Indian culture. We must therefore acknowledge the blind spot in the creole model, which concentrates too much focus on people of African descent while paying insufficient attention to the contributions of people of Indian descent to the creolization process. In the case of Guyana, however, given that the country has a greater number of Indo-Guyanese than any other group, there is not as much assimilation taking place for specifically Hindu or Muslim rituals, although other racial groups are knowledgeable about celebrations such as Matikor, Eid al-Fitr, and Phagwah.

Nigel Bolland attempts to show how the creole model can be used in a dialectical manner. He argues:

> The dialectical analysis of society draws attention to the interrelated and mutually constitutive nature of "individual," "society," and "culture," and of human agency and social structure. Dialectical theory conceives of social life as essentially *practical* activity, and of people as essentially *social* beings. Hence, society consists of the social relations in which people engage in their activities, and is not reducible to individuals. This mutually dependent relationship between social structure and human agency has been referred to as the "dialectics of structuring." (1992, 65)

By using this lens, we can account for multiple forms of domination/subordination as manifested in "status inequalities, defined in terms of race, ethnicity, gender, age and legal status, or a combination of these, as well as class" (Bolland 1992, 65). We are, however, mindful of creolization's shortcomings, as indicated above, despite Bolland's attempt to rehabilitate the concept. The creolization model's failure to address the issue of conflict and its inattention to social class remain problematic.

POSTCOLONIAL THEORY AND THE CREATION OF THE MASALA

In addition to the theoretical perspective of creolization, we will also draw on postcolonial theory to help explain the dynamics of the Indian presence in Guyana and Trinidad. We have already cited the work of George Lamming, and we will continue to draw on his insightful and astute observations. Furthermore, we have found postcolonial theory, with its emphasis on periodization, historicity, culture, and issues of race, ethnicity, and identity, to be particularly useful to our project. We find the theoretical and conceptual framework of Robert Young, Gayatri Spivak, and Brackette Williams to be important to our own work and our analysis of the Indian community in Guyana and Trinidad, even if we do not explicitly cite these authors. The framework of postcolonial theory also gives us the requisite freedom to engage in interdisciplinary analysis. We are both sociologists, but our focus cannot be explained solely through a sociological approach. The range of subjects we engage in this work requires intersecting a sociological approach variously with anthropological, historical, economic, political, and gendered perspectives. Postcolonial theory allows us to navigate such conceptual rapids with a certain degree of confidence.

We will not, however, become stymied by the ponderous question of when the postcolonial era begins because we believe that there is no neat, specific marker of commencement. Rather, if we accept that the postcolonial is a space of resistance, we can then observe the part of the process that begins in the colonial encounter and continues through slavery and indenture, all the way to emancipation, the end of indenture, independence, and beyond. Viewing the postcolonial as a space of resistance allows us to trace the ways—in our particular focus—in which the Indian communities of Guyana and Trinidad have negotiated their own experiences and understanding of identity, citizenship, and belonging.

Earlier, we alluded to Haraksingh's description of Indians in the Caribbean as setting down roots in their adopted homelands. This process is part of the construction of an Indian identity in the region. Identity is constructed on the basis of historical experience, cultural landscape, and social, economic, and political climate; in short, all that affects a people's sense of who they are and the freedom or otherwise to give expression to what sets them apart. Having said the foregoing, however, we concur with the wisdom of Sen when he argues that identities "are robustly plural, and . . . the importance of one identity need not obliterate the importance of others" (2006, 19). It is this plurality of identities that sometimes results in conflict arising out of the social construction of reality. Conflicts surface at times precisely because of the plurality of identities that we embody. Different and competing priorities within our various identities can produce significant discord. For example, given the Anglophone Caribbean's obsession with the game of cricket, indifference to, or lack of loyalty to, the West Indies team is enough to raise suspicion about one's allegiance to the society and the region. Furthermore, when people of Indian descent in the Caribbean appear to demonstrate support for the visiting Indian, Pakistani, or Sri Lankan cricket teams, this perceived national betrayal is condemned vociferously in the pavilions at Bourda Ground in Guyana and the Queen's Park Oval in Trinidad (see Higman 2011 and Lewis 2001a for a discussion of this phenomenon). Perhaps Sen provides us with a way of understanding this apparently conflictual aspect of the Indian identity, not as a betrayal of national or cultural practice but as a response to the competing identity demands for people of Indian descent in Guyana and Trinidad. Sen argues that "the basic seriousness of the disparate pulls—of history, culture, language, politics, profession, family, comradeship, and so on—have to be adequately recognized, and they cannot all be drowned in a single-minded celebration only of community" (2006, 37–38). What these observations point to is the complexity of identity for Indo-Guyanese and Indo-Trinidadians, and for Caribbean people in general. Added to this intricacy is the weight of the postcolonial condition and context against which the challenge of difference and belonging for the Indian community is ever present. We therefore view postcolonial literature and its corresponding discourse to be useful insofar as they provide the complexity and nuance required to appreciate and understand the lived experiences of Indo-Guyanese and Indo-Trinidadians in a comprehensive manner. Works of literature are also particularly helpful in looking at how race is used to negotiate belonging within these postcolonial societies.

THE PREFERENCE OF RACE OVER ETHNICITY

While we are fully aware of the sociological distinction between race and ethnicity, we believe that there is more complexity to this difference than is generally admitted. The sociological literature argues that race is a socially constructed concept that is based on purely physical characteristics. The problem arises when these physical characteristics are then used to predict meaning and behavior that extend beyond the physical to attributes such as intelligence and proclivity for crime or violence. Ethnicity is also believed to be socially constructed but based on cultural characteristics such as religion, geographic location, and historical background. We argue, however, that even though race is often based on purely physical characteristics, we only begin to understand the meaning of those physical markers when we apply cultural interpretations to them. We believe, in other words, that culture is more important in understanding both race and ethnicity and that the distinction might have more to do with society's construction of the two concepts.

In this book, we use the term "race" to refer to the presence of people of Indian descent in Guyana and Trinidad following conventional usage of the term in the Caribbean. We do so for two reasons. First, "race" is the term that is commonly used in the Caribbean to differentiate between people of distinct, recognizable groups. It is perhaps only in academic circles, and among the educated and the middle and upper classes in the Caribbean, that the term "ethnicity" would be used to distinguish between Indo-Caribbean and African Caribbean people. Although the term "ethnicity" may be more appropriate in this context, it would have limited salience outside of the groups identified above. Second, in political and social contexts, ethnicity in both Guyana and Trinidad has most certainly become racialized. This is particularly evident during political campaigns in both countries, when political loyalties, patronage, and access to jobs and valued resources are heavily contested.

GENDER

Much has been written about the issue of gender in the Indian community. Commentators have focused especially on gender roles in the family, and on the role and status of Indian women (Mohammed

2002; Reddock 1998; Niranjana 2011; Nair 2008; Seecharan 2011). *Caribbean Masala* revisits some of this work but also seeks to provide some preliminary exposition of the construction of Indo-Guyanese and Indo-Trinidadian masculinity. The Indian woman has often been portrayed as subservient, domesticated, long suffering, and the upholder of the culture, perhaps less so today than in the past. Jamela Gabriella Hosein and Lisa Outar note that the popular notion of the "Indo-Caribbean woman as Hindu, as passive, as heterosexual, as conservative, as submissive, as guardian of Indian culture via her body and her morality continue to haunt us" (2012, 1). Indian men have been equally stereotyped as violent, drunk, and unwaveringly patriarchal. Hosein (2012, 4) argues that "judgments about masculinity among males relied on control of female sexuality." From within the community, however, Indian men define themselves as dutiful, committed family men, hardworking and purpose driven. This study attempts to shed light on many of these aspects of the construction of masculinity. We are especially interested in teasing out the often unspoken sentiment that African Caribbean masculinity is culturally dominant, in some ways serving as a backdrop against which Indo-Guyanese and Indo-Trinidadian masculinity is defined. We explore some of these issues in the discussions in our focus groups in both countries, in the academic literature addressing the Indian community, and in social science and historical texts, some of which we have already cited.

Given the emphasis that has been placed on Indo-Guyanese and Indo-Trinidadian women, we were determined to examine the construction of Indian masculinity in the two countries. We found that Indian men gave differing responses about how they viewed themselves in terms of their role in the family, the importance of religion, and their place in society. In both countries, we were struck by the way masculinity was constructed in opposition to, and in relation to, the more dominant masculinity of people of African descent. In many of the responses, a comparison with African men was either explicit or implied. Despite the specific cultural differences between the two countries, we recognize the common challenges that Indo-Guyanese and Indo-Trinidadian men—particularly young men—face in negotiating their own development in the current economic climate in which unemployment, the lure of fast money in the drug trade, gang violence, kidnapping, and gender-based violence imperil their daily existence.

CONCLUSION

George Lamming asked an important question many years ago: "[H] ow many books have we had which take us on the inside of Indian life in Trinidad or Guyana?" (1973, 14). Since Lamming raised this question, several texts have appeared addressing precisely what he was most concerned with, if not always on a comparative basis. Such early works as A. R. F. Webber's *Those That Be in Bondage: A Tale of Indian Indentures and Sunlit Western Waters*, Narmal Shewcharan's *Tomorrow Is Another Day*, and Roy Heath's *The Shadow Bride* addressed this lacuna in the Caribbean literary imagination. We endeavor to make a contribution to the question that Lamming raises. The purpose of this book is to provide some cultural context within which readers can develop a broader view of the Indian communities of Guyana and Trinidad, addressing issues of race but going beyond familiar tropes to examine such subjects as ritual, gender, family, and the challenges of modernity. In so doing, we examine not only the extent to which the unrelenting process of creolization has affected descendants of India but also the resilience of this culture in the face of modernizing demands and the process of globalization. In this regard, we found the rituals of Matikor and Phagwah to be important examples of Indian cultural resilience, insofar as one might have anticipated the decline of these practices in the context of modernizing, educated, and urbanized Indian communities in both nations. Far from facing demise, Matikor and Phagwah celebrations remain strong and important rituals in the two countries. Although these rituals have become somewhat creolized in Trinidad, they continue to occupy a space of importance, a stage that many are not prepared to eliminate in their marital and social practices.

The process of globalization is an unyielding process of transformation worldwide, largely responsible for destabilizing some identities while solidifying others. Given our postcolonial concern with identity, we will explore the impact—social, economic, and political—of globalization on the continuing construction and reconstruction of race in the Indian community. Trinidad's complex racial landscape is ripe for analysis, particularly because race impacts how public policy is interpreted. It is a society in which the political mobilization of race has a long tradition, although perhaps not as turbulent as in Guyana. Voting in Trinidad tends to follow fairly strict racial lines; however, there is also considerable mixing at all levels, especially between people of African and Indian descent, that often makes for nuanced expressions of creolization in that society. We explore some of these issues in this text.

Caribbean Masala attempts to merge sociological and anthropological research and methodologies. We collected data in Guyana and Trinidad using focus groups, in-depth interviews, content analysis of newspapers and literature focusing on Indian life and culture in the region, and personal observation. *Caribbean Masala* does not pretend to provide definitive answers to all of the vexing cultural issues raised by our investigation, but it joins the growing literature on the Indian communities of the Caribbean and perhaps, in some small way, responds to George Lamming's concern about getting inside Indian life in Guyana and Trinidad.

1

Theoretical and Historical Sketches of Guyana and Trinidad

Trinidad and Tobago is a twin island republic located in the southeastern corner of the Caribbean. Guyana can be found on the northern coast of the South American mainland, between Venezuela to its west, Suriname to its east, and Brazil to its south. Both countries share a similar colonial history and ethnic makeup, with people of Indian descent representing 39.3 percent of the total population in Guyana and 35 percent in Trinidad. The only other Caribbean country with as significant an Indian presence is Suriname, where Indians, also known as Hindustani, account for 37 percent of the population. In other parts of the Caribbean, such as Saint Vincent, Grenada, Saint Lucia, Martinique, Guadeloupe, and Jamaica, the Indian population is quite small. Our focus on Trinidad and Guyana, then, stems from the social and political significance of the Indian communities in these countries.

Indigenous peoples referred to the vast territory between the Orinoco and Amazon Rivers as "Guiana." The country now known as Guyana has a colonial history not unlike that of Trinidad, marked by imperialist rivalry that played out before the country was ultimately settled by the British. Driven by the myth of El Dorado (the "Golden God") and the rumored existence of abundant gold, Sir Walter Raleigh sailed up the Orinoco in search of this fabled city in 1595. Thereafter, Dutch, French, and other English traders all followed his lead. Captain Lawrence Kemys was the next explorer to venture out, in 1596, followed by Captain Leonard Berrie in 1597. According to one account, crew members on one such expedition returned with tales of so-called natives who had told them of gold mines "so rich that the people of the country powdered themselves with gold-dust" (Swan 1957, 29). Raymond Smith was careful to point out, however, that despite Raleigh's pecuniary interests in El Dorado, he had a broader goal of establishing an English empire between the Amazon and the Orinoco "which would offset Spanish influence in the Americas, and break Spain's trading monopoly" (1962, 13). The Dutch made a claim for a colony that they called Essequibo in 1621. By 1781, the Dutch holdings had been captured by the British. The French later expelled the British, working in concert with the Dutch, and in 1784 the Dutch returned to their former colony. It was not until the Congress of Vienna (1814–1815) that the colonies of Essequibo, Demerara, and Berbice were permanently awarded to and settled by Great Britain. With the consolidation of British colonial rule came the expansion of agriculture and the production of sugar, which in turn expanded the slave trade in African labor. This trade continued into the nineteenth century, when the vicissitudes of sugar production led to the abolition of the trade in human beings in 1807, and total slave emancipation in 1834.

In order to shore up the labor supply, which by now had been depleted by the movement of laborers off the plantations, colonial authorities experimented with Portuguese and Chinese immigrant labor. However, in 1837, John Gladstone—a merchant trader and plantation owner—advised that the dwindling African labor should be replaced by immigrant labor from India. Raymond Smith's observation about the possible future of free labor in this regard is worth noting:

> It had been greatly feared that with emancipation large numbers of
> ex-slaves would remove themselves completely from the coast and go
> off into the bush. This did not happen; the ex-slaves wanted to get off

the plantations but remain in the society, and there was enough land in the form of abandoned plantations to enable them to do so. The establishment of the free Negro villages after emancipation is one of the most remarkable episodes in Guianese history. (1962, 39)

The historical trajectory of indentured labor was somewhat different. The immigration of Indians to Guiana was greater than that of any other immigrant group, continuing from 1838 to 1917. By the time indenture was over, approximately 239,000 Indians had arrived in Guiana. The first arrivals came on board two steamships, the *Whitby* and the *Hesperus*, in May 1839. These indentured workers came mainly from Uttar Pradesh, Bihar, Tamil Nadu, and Bengal. By 1949, 75,547 Indians had returned to their country of origin as a result of a repatriation scheme. Other Indians sought refuge in Guiana's urban environment. However, the great majority of Indians who abandoned the estates "acquired land and became farmers" (Smith 1962, 49). Our focus is on how this group of people adapted to their new circumstances, how they retained and modified their own customs, rituals, and cultural peculiarities in this new environment, and how they continue to negotiate the contours of heritage and contemporary demands in the Republic of Guyana.

COLONIAL RESISTANCE AND POSTCOLONIAL GUYANA

The introduction of indentured Indian workers in Guyana altered the racial makeup of society, which has had lasting effects on the country. Gordon Lewis (1968, 260) notes that one of contemporary Guyana's main problems is to integrate successfully the different racial factions into a common culture. Here, we will briefly sketch Guyana's problematic social and political history.

The early, formalized opposition to colonialism in Guyana came in the form of a coalition of African and Indo-Guyanese in a group called the Political Affairs Committee (PAC). This group raised the consciousness of the Guyanese populace to the problems posed by British colonialism. In 1950, the PAC was formally constituted as a new political party, the People's Progressive Party (PPP), "replacing the old racialist organizations of the East Indian Association and the League of Coloured Peoples" (Lewis 1968, 270). Martin Carter's description of the scope and challenges of this nationalist project is worth citing here:

> [T]he People's Progressive Party was formed in 1950 and immediately started agitating for every imaginable type of social and economic form. It was an agitation that was comparatively undisciplined, but which had the terrific merit of being violently sincere. And the response it had from the people of the country was overwhelming. Because here for the first time you had people not traditionally associated with politics coming into the open and openly demanding an end to the past and the beginning of a new day. (2000, 86)

Unfortunately, this biracial coalition did not last very long.

> The Party successfully contested the first general elections, under universal adult suffrage in 1953. They won 51 percent of the popular vote and had captured 18 of the 24 seats in parliament. Both Britain and the US quickly grew wary of Cheddi Jagan's socialist aspirations, his pro-Soviet stance, and his radical rhetoric against colonialism and imperialism. One should bear in mind that this was at the height of the cold war, and that in the US the communist witch hunt led by Senator Joseph McCarthy was well on its way. The American disapproval, in conjunction with a less than sanguine [Winston] Churchill administration in London, led to the suspension of the Guyanese constitution, a mere 135 days after the elections were held. In 1955, long-ignored and growing tensions between Cheddi Jagan and Forbes Burnham could no longer be contained. Indeed, matters reached a breaking point, and the split in the leadership took place, with Burnham leaving the party to form the PNC [People's National Congress]. (Lewis 2001a, 100–101)

Martin Carter later lamented this development when he observed that what had started as a popular movement against colonialism and imperialism "degenerated into a fight not for power, not for a social revolution, but for succession" (2000, 90). The split in the PPP was made along clearly demarcated racial lines, with the sugar- and rice-field Indian workers siding with the Indo-Guyanese leader, Cheddi Jagan, and the urban working-class and middle-class people of African descent aligning themselves with the African Guyanese leader Forbes Burnham.

The racial division hardened over the years, with the PNC and Burnham controlling the political apparatus from 1964 to 1985, kept in office by a series of well-publicized cases of vote rigging. Burnham died in office in 1985, and the PNC's reign ended in 1992, when Jagan returned to power. The highly charged issue of race, then, accounts for the nearly constant competition between people of African and Indian descent, vying for scarce resources, political patronage, and privilege. This primary conflict between Indians and Africans tends to structure the racial relations of other groups in Guyanese society, namely Portuguese, Chinese, and Amerindian.

Not much changed in racial terms when the PPP took over in 1992, led first by Cheddi Jagan, who died in 1997. His wife, Janet Jagan, replaced him as president and held office for two years. Her death in 2009 marked the end of a political era of early nationalist leaders in Guyana. Janet Jagan was succeeded by Bharrat Jagdeo (1999–2011), who, after serving two terms in office, was replaced by party stalwart Donald Ramotar (2011–2015). The PPP retained power until May 16, 2015, when a coalition party made up of former members of the PPP and PNC along with some political newcomers formed A Partnership for National Unity/Alliance for Change. The new president, David Granger, heads APNU/AFC. Granger is a retired brigadier and commander of the Guyana Defense Force; he was also national security adviser to President Desmond Hoyte in 1990. There is some indication, as projected in public statements, that the Granger administration will make efforts to bridge the racial divide, as also evidenced by the appointment of Moses Nagamootoo, who is of Tamil ancestry, as prime minister. It is too early to tell how successful this government will be in healing the country's deep racial divisions, which have been politicized from the colonial era to the present, but an air of hope and expectation of change has become apparent in contemporary Guyana.

EARLY SETTLEMENT: THE CASE OF TRINIDAD

Columbus dubbed the large island in the southeastern corner of the Caribbean "La Isla de la Trinidad" ("the Island of the Trinity") on his third voyage to the region. The Spaniards initially settled the island; however, they soon lost interest in favor of the more extensive sources of gold in South and Central America. The Spaniards gave permission to the French to use the island, but only when it was taken over by the English in 1797 was it fully incorporated into the global sugar economy. Under English rule, Tobago was administratively added to Trinidad as a twin island territory. Sugar production in Trinidad came much later than it did to the more established plantation economies of Jamaica and Barbados, and it depended on African slave labor. As late as 1812, there were only seventy-eight thousand people in Trinidad, but about 75 percent were slaves. And a significant proportion of these were African-born slaves rather than slaves born in the Caribbean (Higman 1978). After emancipation in 1834, as in Guiana, Britain resorted to Indian indentured labor to work its plantations. Between 1845 and 1917, 147,592 indentured immigrants came to Trinidad from India, again primarily from Uttar Pradesh and Bihar. Their settlement patterns, their acquisition of land offered as an enticement to forgo returning to India, the contractor system in the cocoa industry, the Presbyterian Church, the rise of trade unions, and party politics were to have a profound impact on how they reproduced their social identities in contemporary Trinidad.

The socioeconomic and political structures manifested in contemporary Trinidad are the result of historical processes in the region, primarily stemming from the plantation system (Ryan 1972). Colonial Trinidad was setup to serve the economic and political needs of Europeans. The ruling class of colonial Trinidad was European, and society was governed with the interests of both the ruling class and the colonial government in mind (Williams 1969). The social structure of early Trinidad reflected its colonial status. Society was stratified according to color, race, and class with whites at the top and blacks and Indians at the bottom (Brereton 1972). In colonial Trinidad, Indo-Trinidadians developed a community separate from the rest of the society, with its own cultural norms and values. The British determined the hegemonic culture of colonial Trinidad, and the cultural norms established by this group were accepted (some reluctantly) by many of the freed Africans: "The dominant culture was essentially European, in fact British. It was the middle class, materialistic culture of Victorian Britain" (Brereton 1972, 157). The value system of the society was also heavily influenced by Western Christianity; "there was a general acceptance by Creoles, white and black, of European Christian norms in language, dress and religion although alternative systems co-existed" (Ramesar 1974, 4). But, for the most part, Indo-Trinidadians did not participate in this Western value system.

Spatial isolation resulted in the separation of Indo-Trinidadians from the rest of society (Campbell 1972). This physical isolation was compounded by the religion they practiced. The majority were either Hindus or Muslims, who were considered heathen by the authorities (Brereton 1985). The jobs that Indo-Trinidadians performed on the plantation were shunned by African Trinidadians. "The indenture status itself contributed to the unfavorable images of the 'coolie.' Africans once at the bottom of the social scale, now had an easily recognizable class to which they could feel superior" (Brereton 1985, 30).

Indo-Trinidadians were also hostile to African Trinidadians. They felt that Africans were vulgar and savage. Because of the color of the Africans' skin and the texture of their hair, Indo-Trinidadians equated them with the followers of the demon god Ravan from the Hindu Ramayana. (The Ramayana tells of an epic battle fought between Ram and Ravan. The latter, whose followers were all dark-skinned, kidnapped Ram's wife, setting off the conflict.) In fact, Indo-Trinidadians felt that contact with Africans would pollute the Indian race (Ryan 1972).

The transient position of Indians gave some the incentive to save their money to return home. Indeed, Indians made many deposits in the Trinidad Government Savings Bank (Ramesar 1974). Few, however, returned to India. To retain labor on the island, colonial authorities offered land to Indians. A significant number of Indians took advantage of the contractor system in the cocoa industry to obtain land, or they purchased it outright (Lawrence 1985). Land ownership enabled them to establish a small, independent agricultural peasantry as well as to set up small retail businesses. In this early period, the Indian community in Trinidad had begun to stake its claim to a position in local society.

African Trinidadians during this period, however, sought upward mobility through education and employment opportunities in lower-level white-collar jobs and in the professions, with few working in agriculture or commerce (Brereton 1972). Indo-Trinidadians initially shunned education. Many of them were of the belief that the colonial, Christian education that was made available to them was a threat to their cultural identity. During this time, people of Indian descent were being pressured to convert to Christianity. Certain types of jobs were essentially closed to those who were not Christian, namely jobs in the teaching profession and in the civil service. Indians were also very suspicious of the Presbyterian missions, who sought to convert them to Christianity while providing them with access to education. There was often a certain resentment toward this religious imperialism, which is captured in Harold Sonny Ladoo's unlikely scenario in which a young Indo-Trinidadian, Poonwa, seeks revenge on the Canadian missionaries who had taught him in school. He devises a plan to open a Hindu mission in Canada. He is sure that history will remember him for it:

> In my Mission, all children will have to learn the Hindi alphabet. They will study only Indian History and Hindi Literature. They will have to dress like East Indians. Then I will build more schools and open Hindu temples for the white people to worship the Aryan gods. I will push hard. My Mission so help me God is to make white people good Hindus. I am going to make them feel that their culture is inferior; that the colour of their skin can justify their servitude. Within a few decades I will teach them to mimic Indian ways. Then I will let them go to exist without history. I will make East Indians buy up all their lands and claim all their beaches. Then I will drain all their national wealth and bring it to Tola. In this way I can make East Indians a superior people. (1974, 77–78)

Beneath the improbability and humor of Poonwa's enterprise is of course the deep psychological pain of the inferiorization inflicted by the Canadian Presbyterian tutelage and cultural imposition. Ladoo also clearly forces the reader to come to terms with ideas of colonial revolt against conditions of oppression. This revolt against colonialism depends partly on investing in the benefits of an education. Indo-Trinidadians became interested in education in the post-1930 period when, amid discussion about universal adult suffrage, it was suggested only those who were literate in English would be allowed to vote. Many unaided Indian schools emerged, and Indo-Trinidadians began to recognize the advantages of education, some even going so far as to undergo religious conversion to gain access to it: "East Indian converts to Christianity soon realized how socially and economically rewarding was their acceptance of baptism and membership in the Canadian Presbyterian Mission" (Premdas and Sitahal 1991, 345).

The political structures and practices of the colonial period also reinforced the status quo. After World War I, the black working class called for political reforms, demanding responsible government, full democracy, and trade union representation. By and large, the Indo-Trinidadian population did not support these reforms because they feared African Trinidadian domination. An investigation by the Wood Commission (1921–1922) resulted in a limited franchise in which the major political player was the Trinidad Workingmen's Association led by Captain Arthur Andrew Cipriani. This still, however, did not allow for widespread electoral participation, and trade unions remained illegal. Due to constant agitation, the Trade Union Ordinance passed in 1932, legitimizing trade unions.

By the 1930s, new leaders had begun to emerge who were more radical than Cipriani. One such leader was Tubal Uriah "Buzz" Butler. Butler, of African descent, was born on the island of Grenada. He organized and led a series of strikes in the oil fields (which comprised mainly African Trinidadian workers) and in the sugar industry (which was mainly made up of people of Indian descent). The strikes and labor riots of 1937 set in motion processes for the growth of trade

unions and the establishment of universal adult suffrage, which led
to self-government and, in turn, party politics.

COLONIAL RESISTANCE AND POSTCOLONIAL TRINIDAD

Following the release of the Moyne Commission report in 1945,
major political and constitutional reform was enacted the next year.
Universal suffrage was granted to everyone over the age of twenty-
one, and a new Legislative Council was installed. The 1950 elections
saw the emergence of an alliance between Butler and a group of Indo-
Trinidadian politicians in an attempt to break the trend of Africans
and Indians facing off against each other in elections. Their aim was
to "revolutionize the distribution of political and economic power
in Trinidad and Tobago" (Ryan 1972, 89). Butler's party won the
single largest block of seats—six—of which four were held by Indo-
Trinidadians. The governor and the colonial authorities, however, were
concerned about the radical orientation of Butler's party, and it was
no surprise when none of the party's elected members were asked to
be on the Executive Council.

The 1956 elections saw the emergence of the People's National
Movement (PNM), led by Eric Williams, as a political force. The
People's Democratic Party (PDP), which was essentially an arm of
the Hindu community, emerged to oppose the PNM. The 1956 elections for the first time saw political parties organized purely along
lines of race. From 1956 to 1986, the PNM was to have continuous
control over the state. This situation over an extended period created
the perception that African Trinidadians would control the political
machinery, and Indo-Trinidadians and whites the economic sphere.
With control of the state came control over state resources and jobs
in the public sector, and few Indo-Trinidadians were employed in
this sector. They were concentrated in agriculture and independent
small business.

The PNM government sought to encourage modernization through
the development of industry. Modeling its efforts on the works of
W. Arthur Lewis and his notion of "industrialization by invitation,"

the government sought to diversify the economy and encourage the private sector to invest. There was also reform in Crown land use for agriculture after independence in 1963. The land reform measures did not result in the improvement of agricultural production. Similarly, the new industries were capital intensive and had little labor absorption capacity. Indeed, the failure of the development strategy resulted in the Black Power upheavals of 1970. Furthermore, the technology employed made little use of local raw materials and had few organic linkages with Trinidad's economy. Given the colonial legacy of capital in the hands of a white colonial elite, it is no surprise that instead of this process reducing inequality, which it was intended to do, it in fact allowed the local elites to consolidate and further entrench their position of power and privilege in society (Craig 1982).

The Black Power upheavals, coupled with a windfall in state revenue owing to an increase in oil prices, allowed the government to change its development strategy. It increased its ownership and participation in the economy and sought to provide financial support to small and large businesses to diversify ownership. Changes in the social structure came with the opening up of the money economy and increased government spending on education. Indo-Trinidadians posed the first real threat to the dominant white business elite. They sought to use self-employment as a means of mobility and looked inward to protect themselves from perceived discrimination in the wider society. A number of other factors facilitated this process, including the availability of land and the prevalence of large families who pooled their resources and could rely on cheap and often unpaid labor. These factors provided an excellent platform for them to take advantage of the opportunities that resulted from increased state spending. By the early 1970s, Indo-Trinidadians controlled large portions of the construction, hardware, and retail industries and some sectors of the manufacturing industry (Ramsaran 1993).

The second factor leading to changes in the social structure was expanded state spending on education, all the way to the tertiary level. Despite the emerging inequality even in the schools, many people who earlier would not have had access to education gained access. An increasing number of people of Indian descent took advantage of this opportunity. In particular, more Indo-Trinidadian women began to attend school, which would significantly reduce the power of the patriarchal system prevalent in Indo-Trinidadian homes. Greater Indo-Trinidadian participation in education led to increased competition for jobs in the professional and public sectors, which were seen as the domain of persons of African descent. This development had a direct impact on Trinidad's occupational hierarchy, and Indo-Trinidadian women enjoyed higher levels of mobility than all other groups in society (Reddock 1998).

The collapse of oil prices in the 1980s caused the country's economy to flounder. The government was forced to reduce its expenditures and devalue the currency, resulting in increased inflation and unemployment. Some disenchanted elements of the African and Indo-Trinidadian middle class along with French-Creole citizens formed the Organization for National Reconstruction (ONR) to challenge the PNM. In the 1986 elections, the ONR allied with the United Labour Front (ULF) under the banner of the National Alliance for Reconstruction (NAR) under the leadership of A. N. R. Robinson, and for the first time since Trinidad gained independence the PNM was defeated.

The NAR was forced to make unpopular economic decisions. The government adopted the neoliberal model in an attempt to bring its recurrent expenditures in line with revenue, reduced the wages and benefits of civil servants, and suspended cost-of-living allowances (most recipients were Trinidadians of African descent). In addition, many of the "make-work" schemes that the state had used to alleviate poverty in the past had to be suspended, resulting in increased unemployment and discontent in the society. Infighting between Indo- and African Trinidadians in what was perceived as a competition for the spoils of political office resulted in the fracturing of the NAR. Basdeo Panday and his ULF supporters argued that the African Trinidadian elements within the NAR were simply perpetuating the discrimination that had been practiced by the PNM. The "Panday faction" was expelled from the party, and they reconstituted the ULF under the banner of the United National Congress (UNC). These problems were complicated by an attempted coup by a militant Islamic sect—the Jamaat al Muslimeen—in 1990.

In 1991, the PNM was elected back into office, and relative normalcy returned to political and social life. Trinidadians perceived that balance was restored, with the African Trinidadians in control of the political arena and the Indo-Trinidadians dominating the private sector. The PNM continued its neoliberal policies of the past; while the new prime minister, Patrick Manning, sought to rekindle the flames of the "old PNM" of Eric Williams, the party was unable to achieve that goal. One of the major problems was that, with the impetus of structural adjustment programs, the economy was growing, but little of that growth was getting to the people. Further, the PNM began to have internal problems and called early elections in 1995. As a result of this election, Basdeo Panday, with the support of a political party based in Tobago that was led by former prime minister A. N. R. Robinson, was sworn in as the country's first Indo-Trinidadian prime minister.

With an Indo-Trinidadian political party controlling the state, some perceived that Indians would now completely dominate both the economic and political sectors. Moreover, new government policies deepened the process of private sector–led development. Some even feared that Indo-Trinidadian political control of the private sector would allow the Indian business sector to "suck the country dry"—exploit the economy for its own narrow interests. Some popular culture outlets cried out about corruption, and race inevitably became the lens through which the discontent was articulated.

In 2001, Panday's UNC, facing dissent within its ranks over allegations of corruption, went to the polls, which resulted in an 18–18 hung parliament. Robinson, who was serving as president of the country, asked the PNM to form a new government. Another election was held one year later, and the PNM, under Manning, won a two-seat majority. The PNM also won the elections of 2007, but allegations of corruption and uncontrolled crime were foremost among their problems. In 2010, Kamla Persad-Bissessar wrestled power in the UNC away from the party's old patriarch, Basdeo Panday. The PNM called an early election that year, and the People's Partnership (PP), a coalition of opposition parties including the UNC, won the election; Persad-Bissessar, an Indo-Trinidadian woman, became Trinidad's first female prime minister. This achievement enabled a significant advancement for the status of women in general in Trinidad, but in particular for Indo-Trinidadian women. Indian men historically believed that women belonged at home taking care of the children, subservient to male power. Persad-Bissessar's political achievement did not eliminate the Indo-Trinidadian patriarchy but significantly weakened its power.

The PP government largely reproduced the divisions that existed in the NAR, with competition for positions of authority between African and Indo-Trinidadian elements; allegations of bias against persons of African descent and corruption resulted in the return of the PNM to power in 2015. The PNM, however, has not been able to broaden its base, and it remains essentially an African Trinidadian party. It is within this context that the contemporary contestation over belonging and identity takes place.

THEORIZING ABOUT THE INDIAN PRESENCE IN THE CARIBBEAN

Making sense of the experience of Indo-Caribbean people is a task that is fraught with theoretical traps and pitfalls. Indeed, using any one single grand theory to explain Caribbean societal structures and forms is bound to be inadequate because of the many foundations upon which the Caribbean is constructed, including African, European, Asian, and Amerindian. Scholars have taken many approaches to analyzing the dynamics of Caribbean societies. Two approaches that have been central in these efforts are the "plural" and the "creole" models. The two models are premised on opposite ends of a continuum: cultural persistence on one end and cultural mixing on the other.

Michael G. Smith, in a series of publications drawing on the works of J. S. Furnivall, argues that Caribbean societies are culturally and socially plural. His premise is that culture can only be investigated by looking at the institutional frameworks that dictate action in these societies, because institutions determine set forms of activities, grouping rules, ideas, and values: "The institutions of a people's culture form the matrix of their social structure, simply because the institutional system defines the sanctions and persistent forms of social life. To define the social structure, we must therefore analyze the institutional system" (Smith 1960, 767). For Smith, Caribbean societies are made up of distinct and separate cultural groups, each having its own unique institutional arrangements for all aspects of social life. He suggests that these societies are held together by force, by a dominant minority. Despite Smith's recognition that power is a central factor in keeping these societies together, he argues that these cultural groups are not arranged in any hierarchy among themselves but that status differentiations are found within each group. In a subsequent reformulation of the model, Smith introduces the concept of "differential incorporation," arguing that different groups in a society are differentially incorporated into the public domain (Reddock 1998). Susan Craig (1982) correctly notes that Smith theorizes about an "imaginary homogenous" society that fails to take into consideration issues related to gender and cross-culturation between different groups, or the foundation of power that keeps the hegemonic group in place. Furthermore, the class dimension, which tends to lie behind the more prominent race dimension in multiethnic societies, is completely left out of the plural model.

As described earlier, Brathwaite's use of interculturation and acculturation in the process of creolization goes a long way to explain the dominance of European cultural forms practiced in the Caribbean. Reddock (1998) demonstrates the usefulness of this approach to understanding the Caribbean when considering Trinidad. By the early 1900s, she argues, there were three distinct cultures in Trinidad in competition with each other for hegemony. First was the dominant white European culture, whose members dominated the state and held economic power. Then there was creole culture, which was still emerging and contained many elements of European and African culture. Finally there was the newly introduced Indian culture, which arrived in Trinidad from 1845 to 1917. With the rise of the African Trinidadian middle class, European culture was partially absorbed into the creole culture, which together formed the new hegemonic culture. According to Reddock, "that culture was formed through imitation but also through the native creation and indigenization of African and European cultural forms which until recently became the accepted culture of the society" (1998, 418). Two schools of thought attempt to incorporate Indo-Trinidadian culture in this scenario, one suggesting that Indo-Trinidadian culture remains separate and distinct, the other that, over time, the Indian community has been assimilated into the dominant "Creole/Euro-Christian culture" (Reddock 1998, 418). In the process of globalization, Indo-Trinidadians are becoming more absorbed in the mainstream culture while at the same time using elements of Indo-Trinidadian culture to resist that process, and the creole model can best account for this development.

In a similar fashion, the process of creolization has had some of the same effects in Guyana. Raymond Smith, for example, notes that African Guyanese, mixed-race people, and whites "all came to share a common conception of colonial society; a conception in which things English and 'white' were valued highly whilst things African and 'black' were valued lowly" (1962, 41). Smith further notes that even when some Indo-Guyanese moved away from the estates, they did not become automatically assimilated into creole society (1962, 49). While social cleavages occurred more or less naturally in Trinidad, a number of historical and political factors, including the impact of colonial policy, resulted in a different cultural dynamic in Guyana. Here, Indo-Guyanese outnumbered African Guyanese, although the majority still found itself dominated culturally by African creole influences. While Indo-Guyanese were the majority on the rice and sugar plantations, African Guyanese had a notable presence in the civil service and what Walter Rodney described as the "uniformed professions." Meanwhile, Guyanese of Chinese and Portuguese descent tended to operate in the business community on all levels, and some members of both these communities were eventually absorbed into the white elite. A coalition of Indo- and African Guyanese elites forged a new type of alliance, which led to the creation of a successful national political party in the early 1950s, but the alliance had collapsed by 1955. The resulting racial polarization between the two communities, alluded to earlier, still continues to structure political participation, patronage, the distribution of resources, and the exercise of power, while casting a pall on race relations in Guyana.

Bolland attempts to show how the creole model can be potentially used in a dialectical way. He argues: "the dialectical analysis of society draws attention to the interrelated and mutually related constitutive nature of the 'individual,' 'society,' and 'culture,' and of human agency and society and social structure.... This mutually dependent relationship between social structure and human agency have been referred to as the 'dialectics of structuring'" (Bolland 1992, 65). By using this perspective, he argues, we can account for multiple forms of domination/subordination as manifested in "status inequalities, defined in terms of race, ethnicity, gender, age and legal status, or a combination of these, as well as class" (Bolland 1992, 65). Subsequent analysis reveals even more complexity as in evident in the work of Édouard Glissant, who seeks to differentiate between creolization and *métissage*:

> [C]reolisation is not uprooting, loss of sight, suspension of being; errantry is not wandering; diversity is not delusion. When we speak of creolisation, we don't only mean *métissage*—cross breeding—because creolisation adds something new to the components that participate in it.... [C]reolisation is unpredictable, whereas you can more or less calculate the immediate result of cross-breeding. Creolisation opens up a radically new dimension of reality, not a mechanical combination of components where you could value percentages; therefore creolisation, which overlaps with linguistic projection, does not produce direct synthesis, but results [in] something else, another way. (2011, 13–14)

He goes on to argue that this process is neither linear nor authoritative but rather rooted in discontinuity, ambiguity, and open-endedness because it involves "imagining and recreating from traces or recall." For Glissant, then, it is in these interstices that something new emerges from the dynamic mixing. "So ambiguity, discontinuity, trace remembering creolisation with its unpredictable results are not signs of weakness. They contribute to this unprecedented conception of identity that I have been discussing" (Glissant 2011, 18).

Kavyta Raghunandan, addressing the notion of hyphenated identity, argues that "the identification of Indian Trinidadians must, therefore be understood as dynamically negotiated in response to cultural and political contexts" (2012, 6). Moreover, she opposes the use of hyphenated identities because they tend to be rooted purely in the ethnic experience rather than in the true, lived reality defined more intricately along lines of gender and religion. She suggests that it is false to assume that an Indian's creolization indicates assimilation into the dominant creole culture, as "it is presumed that the 'Indian' is [a] passive recipient of another culture" (2012, 13). We argue, however, that there is nothing inherently built into the process of creolization that suggests that Indo-Caribbean people are automatically assimilated into the dominant African creole culture. Rather, the process can go in the other direction such that the dominant culture itself changes to include elements of Indo-Caribbean culture. So, instead of Indo-Trinidadians or Indo-Guyanese assimilating into African Creole culture, that dominant culture itself is changing by assimilating facets of minority cultures. This dynamic is essentially a political and cultural process, with gender, class, and religion having a profound impact. Raghunandan proposes the concept of "douglarization," which avoids the Afrocentric bias of the word "creole" and allows for a feminist identity among Indo-Trinidadian women. Renaming the very act of "mixing" does not, however, guarantee the elimination of an inherent bias. A *dougla* is a person with half-Indian, half-African parentage, but that does not mean that both cultures are equally represented in that person. Some *douglas* may be raised in a cultural environment that is predominantly African, and this cultural context can have significant influence on the identities of those individuals. Kamala Kempadoo's discussion of the *dougla* (*dogla* in Guyana) is a useful historical and explanatory observation:

> Originating from Hindi to signify a "crossbreed" between castes, the result of an inter-caste relationship, the name [dogla] has undergone some variation in the Caribbean and today refers to a person of mixed Indian and non-Indian (usually African) descent. It is a part of the general vocabulary of these three South Caribbean [Guyana, Suriname, Trinidad] territories.
>
> The name "Dogla" traditionally carries a derogatory connotation, and it is not only by Hindus that such a person is considered an outcast or impure. Afro-Guyanese also hold a low regard for Doglas, and

the term is often used to insult or to reject those of us of "mixed race."
Whether this pejorative usage has to do with a specific history of race
relation is subject to further inquiry. However, besides the specific
label in the Caribbean, the categorization of people of mixed race as
contaminated, impure and ethnic bastards occurs in other societies,
pointing to a phenomenon which has less to do with the type of mix
and more to do with notions of "race" and "ethnic purity." (1999, 104)

In contemporary Guyana and Trinidad, the term *dougla* has undergone even more of a semantic shift whereby much of the original
derogatory insinuation has been replaced, with few exceptions, by
notions of sexual desirability. At the popular level, the common
interpretation is that the *dougla* has taken the best features from
her African and Indian ancestry and hence has become more sexually attractive to others. We are decidedly not concerned here with
the social or sexual desirability of the *dougla* but cite persons in
this racial category as subjects of a process of mixing that has to
be considered as part of a broader orientation toward creolization.
Additionally, the concept of the *dougla* can easily be used to reinforce hierarchies of color gradations—measuring lighter and darker
skin tones—analogous to the gradations of whiteness that race theo-
ries associate with social class and national origin. Race remains a
central variable around which identity and the interpretation of
public policy are articulated, especially when they involve access to
the resources of the state.

Specifically, the creole model is also amenable to accounting for
gender issues and women's subordination, at the center of which is the
notion of patriarchy. Gerda Lerner (1986) argues that patriarchy is the
result of a historical process, created over time, and that its impact varies based on age, class, and race/ethnicity. Patricia Mohammed (1998),
continuing along the same line of reasoning as Reddock, argues that
in colonial Trinidad there were three patriarchies competing with
each other: a dominant white patriarchy, a "creole" patriarchy that was
emerging among the Africans, and a patriarchy that existed among
the newly arrived population from India. With the emergence of
the African Trinidadian middle class and the rise of the nationalist

movement, African and creole merged as the dominant patriarchy, and the Indo-Trinidadian patriarchy stood as its rival.

Jamela Gabriella Hosein (2012) examines the intersection of modernity (which is heavily influenced by Bollywood and US standards of modernity) and creolization in the experience of young Indo-Trinidadian women. She argues that these women negotiate their identity using multiple inputs including postcolonial Indian modernity, Bollywood, European and American notions of metropolitanism, "Indo-Trinidadian . . . modernity and its tensions regarding class, religion, geography, respectability and women's sexual freedom, as seen in debates regarding chutney music; and . . . creole-modernity, best exemplified by Carnival's visible staging of the nation" (Hosein 2012, 3). Drawing on Niels Sampath (1993), who argues that creolization is an instrument of "masculine power," Hosein prefers to use modernity to explain identity formation among adolescent Indo-Trinidadian women, since, "[u]nlike creolization, modernity carries multiple meanings, many of which can be acceptably accommodated by Indian girls, providing safe and legitimate access to 'creole modernity'" (Hosein 2012, 8). Creole modernity is taken to indicate the manner in which Western influences are interpreted by Indo-Caribbean people within the context of the African creole Caribbean.

To locate the Indo-Caribbean population within the race, class, and gender dynamic, different authors tend to straddle between cultural persistence on one hand and mixing on the other. Within the context of nation building, there is the tendency to see creolization as a process that involves mainly Africans and Europeans. This conception has led to the idea that the Caribbean nation-state is based on African Caribbean culture, which is itself a creolized form, and therefore African culture has come to represent national culture. Indo-Caribbean populations then found themselves having to compete with "national culture" for legitimacy. The Indo-Caribbean community was seen as outside the nation-building process, since "Indian" culture was not seen as part of the national culture. Indeed, many prominent Indo-Caribbean leaders in the political and cultural arena sought to define the Indo-Caribbean population not based on the similarities between themselves and the African Caribbean population, but between themselves and the "purity" of the Indian culture and identity that they brought from India. Viranjini Munasinghe, looking specifically at the case of Trinidad, suggests that, although there is a tendency to see the African Trinidadian community as "creolized," the Indo-Trinidadian community has also exhibited aspects of creolization, while not necessarily adopting African creole forms of expression.

> Indo-Trinidadians too may be considered creolized without suggestion that they are assimilating into Afro-Creole cultural patterns. . . . Indo-Trinidadians' creative capacity to forge novel cultural forms in the New World by piecing together diverse elements tends to be eclipsed in popular and academic representations of Indo-Trinidadians as bearers of a particularistic Indian culture or assimilators into wider Euro- and Afro-Creole patterns. (Munasinghe 2001, 8)

As such, although "Indianness" in the Caribbean context may be associated with historical connections from South Asia, it is in fact creolized forms of "Indianness" that are produced within the specific socioeconomic and political contexts of the respective societies.

In an attempt to locate the Indo-Caribbean population within a broader context, one must take into consideration the conditions under which they arrived: the colonial context. But the negotiation of "Indianness" within the Caribbean context more specifically depends on the extent to which one's identity is dependent on the purity of the received view from India, or the extent to which it is a reflection of compromise within the local situation. It is also determined by the position of "Indian culture" vis-à-vis creole culture in the drive toward nationhood. Finally, "Indianness" in this context is also determined by changes that occurred in the post-1980 period, when the region broadly transformed from a state-centered economy to one dictated by the demands of a neoliberal economy and increased globalization.

This negotiation by Indians for space and identity with a dominant hegemonic culture and a changing political economy is not unique to the Caribbean. Vijay Prashad, in *The Karma of Brown Folk* (2000), sought to understand how South Asians negotiated the process in the United States. He also noted a process of mixing and duality.

South Asian integration into US society had to be analyzed against the backdrop of multiculturalism and race in the context of the United States, including the circumstances surrounding their arrival (the bulk of the desis [South Asians] who arrived in the 1960s were highly educated, to combat Soviet advances in space exploration) as well as the prevailing ideology of blacks as "pathological" and a "problem" population. South Asians, or "desis," were seen as a "model minority" in that "many tended to follow an old tradition that groups Indians with whites in a racial family called 'Aryan,' believing that if they are joined in this racial fantasy and can explain this to the bulk of the population, then they would be accepted" (Prashad 2000, 93). This embrace of "whiteness" allowed upwardly mobile desis to argue that they were not "black," similar to arguments articulated by some Hindu groups in Guyana and Trinidad. Prashad argues that "as desis we are used as weapons in the war against black America" (2000, ix). In a 2012 publication entitled *Uncle Swami*, Prashad analyzes how the children of these first-generation desis sought to negotiate their position in the United States. He argues that the identifier of "South Asian American" is not a reference to a place but rather

> to a sense of community among children of parents from various countries in South Asia. . . . The content of their cultural lives might have been different, but the form was the same: South Asian parents, with their robust connections to their homelands and their own ideas of raising children, and American schools and friends, with their own worldviews and expectations. It was this duality that was shared across the students. (Prashad 2012, 13–14)

Prashad locates the process of negotiating desi identity in the United States within the context of global capitalism on the one hand and within the internal US hierarchical ideology of race relations on the other. Looking specifically at how desis negotiated the post-9/11 period, during which every brown person from South Asia was associated with terrorism, he argues that

> the fear factor of "blacks" created the conditions for the construction of the Indian American (and the Asian American in general) as a

model minority, whereas now I argue that is insufficient. It is the face of terror of the "Muslim" alongside antiblack racism that provides the political space for Jewish Americans and Indian (or sometimes Hindu) Americans to mitigate their cultural difference against the mainstream, but critically to put themselves forward as those who, because of their experience with terrorism, become the vanguard of the new, antiterrorist Battleship America. (Prashad 2012, 64)

Indeed, Prashad sees the process of mixing under US multiculturalism not in an osmotic way but rather as being locked into a system that inherently prioritizes European cultures and white supremacy, a system that makes

the comfortable assumption ... that our histories belong—but do not in any way come close to—the untouched (and generally unspoken) superiority of the cultures of Europe (and European culture in the United States). The world of multiculturalism welcomes cultures of other lands (Africa, Asia, Latin America) and puts them up for display. But is unwilling to allow this new cultural recognition to disrupt the contented place of European culture at the top of an unspoken hierarchy. (Prashad 2012, 111–12)

Prashad's argument is not far removed from the problematic nature of the process of mixing in the Caribbean, which is based on racial hierarchies, and where acceptance of the creolization process is fraught with issues of the partial subservience of one's identity.

Another example of the difficulty of integrating cultures is given by Nitasha Tamar Sharma, who discusses how hip-hop is used by some elements of the college-educated desi population:

As the official discourse on difference that impacted structural and funding decisions in universities, multiculturalism impacted desis' college education and identity exploration just as counterhegemonic narratives delivered in rhyme were filling the airwaves. The confluence of these economic policies and political and racial discourses directly affected the way that desi youth understood themselves. (2010, 16)

Drawing on the notion of "cross-fertilization" as well as "cut 'n' mix" identities, Sharma argues that engagement with black culture through hip-hop allows desis to "contest hegemonic desiness, or the expectations that ethnic gatekeepers place on co-ethnics" (2010,11). Combining the common experience of South Asians and blacks with "historical and global processes rooted in colonialism" (2010, 3) allows them to "create new and empowering meanings of 'race' that capture the interplay of identification and distancing by pushing beyond existing national boundaries and racial categories" (2010, 5).

The problematic coexistence of the dominant African creole culture and Indian culture in the Caribbean is central to explaining the location of Indo-Caribbean populations within their particular socioeconomic, political, and gendered spaces. Some have argued that, in essence, the Indo-Caribbean population has remained separate from the African creole population by adopting a plural model and arranging the cultures in hierarchical terms, thus retaining the "purity" that was brought from India. According to Munasinghe, "the division between East Indian and Creole had its origins in colonial history and continues to be a pivotal ideological axiom through which Trinidadians perceive and comprehend their society" (2001, 122). Aisha Khan makes a similar argument, suggesting that the colonial stratification process based on class, race, and color "laid the foundation for a postcolonial society whose hallmark has been ethnic group competition, fostered by class inequalities and state control for certain resources and couched in terms of racial antipathies between Indo- and Afro-Trinidadians" (2004, 9). Although these two arguments were made with respect to Trinidad, a similar argument can be made for Guyana and the relationship between Indo- and African Guyanese. As suggested earlier, when indentured labor was introduced, African Guyanese viewed Indians not merely as interlopers but as devaluing the worth of their free labor and as representing a source of competition. In short, whatever difficulty exists today between these two groups in Guyana was fomented in the colonial process of divide and conquer and subsequently mobilized by politicians for their own advantage.

In both Guyana and Trinidad, groups have developed views that differentiate people in the local context: "In Trinidad, as in Guyana, a generalized system of beliefs based on the notion of fundamental difference between Creole and East Indians prevails and is expressed mainly in the form of ethnic stereotypes" (Munasinghe 2001, 128). These stereotypes inform how different groups perceive each other. As such, Indo-Trinidadians and Indo-Guyanese view their African compatriots as lazy, prone to womanizing, and "just like to fete," while African Trinidadians and African Guyanese view Indians as clannish, corrupt, wife-abusing alcoholics, overly frugal and prone to suicide.

In addressing the notion of "Indian identity," both Indo-Trinidadians and Indo-Guyanese ask whether their respective identities reflect the "purity" of their Indian ancestry. In both spaces, the Indian community must determine the extent to which they want to associate their "Indianness" with India, or with the nation-state in which they were born.

Much of Caribbean nationalism is rooted in the notion of creole culture; how, then, does one create an Indian identity in such a context? Tejaswini Niranjana (2006, 33) argues that Indianness in the Caribbean, although informed by practices in India, was driven by the need to differentiate itself from other races, namely African Trinidadians and by extension African Guyanese. "Attempting to erase difference with India rather than to mark it, Indians assert a racial similarity in relation to the 'mother country' and a racial difference in relation to the politically dominant group in their nation-state." In a sense, then, while some Indian elites stress their continuity with India, in reality they are creolizing their "Indianness" in order to differentiate themselves from the African Caribbean community.

Another major factor that has influenced the notion of "Indianness" in both Guyana and Trinidad is the competition for political power. In both countries, political parties are formed along racial lines, and the postcolonial state was constructed along African Caribbean notions of nationalism. In the case of Trinidad, the organizing principle for the new nation-state was African creole culture. Referring specifically to Trinidad, Munasinghe notes, "the thirty years of PNM rule left behind two principal legacies: the identification of the state with the cultural history of Creoles, that is, with those of African ancestry; and their proclivity to mute ethnic differences for the good of the nation" (2001, 220). Similarly, the political domination of the essentially African-based PNC government led by Forbes Burnham also left an undeniably African mark on the political culture of Guyana. An only slightly different orientation was annunciated by Burnham's successor, Desmond Hoyte, in the period 1985–1992. Cheddi Jagan's return to power in 1992 marked a break in African predominance in Guyanese politics.

Some of these racial tensions also play themselves out in gender relations. Gender is an important element with respect to claiming "Indianness" in the Caribbean. For both male and female Indo-Trinidadians and Indo-Guyanese, gender is usually defined in opposition to African Trinidadian and African Guyanese masculinity and femininity. Moreover, as with racial formations, gender identities are formed against a backdrop of colonial stereotypes. Looking specifically at Indian femininity in Trinidad, Niranjana notes that "not only is the Indian woman in Trinidad formed by discourses of colonialism; she is also shaped by the nationalist discourses in India" (2006, 53). The stress on purity, beauty, and submissiveness to the patriarchy is noted in contrast to the African Trinidadian woman, who is presented as the jamette, "seen as vulgar, promiscuous, loud and disruptive" (Niranjana 2006, 82). The contestation of Indian femininity continues today. With changes in access to education and the weakening of Indo-Trinidadian patriarchy, Indo-Trinidadian femininity is being redefined, particularly in the public space, as evidenced by increased female participation in chutney and carnival culture, the latter seen in the past as part of African creole culture. Many have complained about the "vulgarity" of Indo-Trinidadian women "wining" (gyrating) during carnival and in chutney fetes. Niranjana observes that "the analysis of contemporary Trinidadian discourses of East Indian women's sexuality has to be placed within a framework of the predominantly biracial society of the island. Indian tradition (and Indian women) in Trinidad come to be defined as those who are not, or cannot be allowed to become, African" (2006, 123). In Guyana, Indian women have become increasingly involved in intellectual circles, progressive women's organizations, and professional spheres, and they have held various ministerial portfolios in government. Hosein (2012) points to the fact that young, middle-class Indo-Trinidadian women are adopting European and American notions of modernity, which she refers to as "creole modernity," while not forfeiting their "Indianness." She concludes: "These girls seek status through both Indo-Trinidadian notions of honor and modern notions of reputation or freedom from shame associated with whiteness and Euro-America, women's education and empowerment and assertive public sexuality" (2012, 19).

Similar to Indo-Trinidadian women, Indo-Trinidadian men's masculinity is defined in relation to African Trinidadian masculinity. Based on colonial stereotypes, African Trinidadian men are defined as "badjohns" (persons given to violent and lawless conduct), prone to short-term thinking, dependent on handouts by the state, lazy, and philandering. Indo-Trinidadian men conversely are defined as industrious and hard working, good with money, and progressive (Munasinghe 2001). We tend to see this as a one-way process. Niranjana correctly points out that "African masculinity . . . has to be shaped alongside and against the Indian, whose masculinity is then delegitimized or becomes bad or violent masculinity" (2006, 131).

All approaches to locating the Indian presence in the Caribbean have wrestled with the issues of race, gender, class, and religion, as well as the vexing notion of "mixing" in some form or fashion, whether mixing top-down (forced and hierarchical), bottom-up (osmotic), or horizontally (nonhierarchical). All of these processes are influenced by history and by changes in the global geopolitical and economic system. It is with these fundamental understandings in mind that we look at race as an identity signifier. The way we understand race and identity has implications for the manner in which public policy is perceived by different racial groups. These considerations in turn influence how Indo-Guyanese and Indo-Trinidadian masculinity is constructed and experienced in the contemporary economic climate of the Caribbean. In the following chapters, we analyze these issues in the context of social change, including how people of Indian descent try to maintain important aspects of their identity in terms of rituals (as in the case of Dig-Dutty/Matikor), race, and gender.

2

Race, Creolization, Globalization, and Public Policy in Trinidad

This chapter focuses on the nexus between globalization, racial identity, and public policy in Trinidad. Specifically, we analyze how racial identity can be used to contest public policies that are enacted to facilitate the globalization process. Generally, during the decolonization process, elites seek to find a common ideology around which they can rally and create their nation-state. In some colonial societies where political parties are organized along racial lines, the organizing nationalist ideology reflects the position of the dominant racial group. In the process of ongoing modernization and globalization, racial groups who perceive themselves to be marginalized within the nation-state, instead of being absorbed into the homogenizing tendencies of the dominant culture, begin more radically to contest the homogenizing currents of globalization. Protest becomes a way to "separate" themselves from the dominant cultural segments. Managing race relations within the context of creolization is not a smooth process, and certain public policy issues provide an arena in which race relations and racial identity issues are contested.

The meaning and application of the concept of "race" has generated serious contention. Race is a social marker that is used to arrange persons and groups into a hierarchical system in which power and the distribution of scarce resources are closely related. The arrangement of racial categories into a hierarchy is an intensely social task influenced by history and by socioeconomic and political factors. Race is socially defined; as such, it incorporates dimensions of cultural constructions. It also engenders certain misconceptions about people that are clearly not based on objective criteria.

Viranjini Munasinghe subsumes race under the concept of ethnicity particularly in colonial and postcolonial contexts. She argues that "since ethnicity more than race speaks to the socially constituted nature of identifications, it can stand as an overarching framework within which race relations are situated" (2001, 13). This is a particularly important point, because certain ethnic features such as dress or religion can become the markers through which racial claims are asserted. In Trinidad, regardless of how we define the term "race," it has had a profound impact on people's self-identity. Historically and today, race is an important variable when considering resource distribution, political participation, public perception, and the interpretation of public policy. This form of identity is also influenced by other variables such as social class, gender, age, and religion. Furthermore, identity is not static but rather evolves over time; racial identity is being creolized, and modernization and globalization provide the structural background against which this evolution takes place.

The topic of globalization has evoked debate among contending ideologies. Those who support the process highlight its positive aspects, namely economic growth. Those who oppose globalization point to the negative dimensions—environmental degradation, loss of jobs, and deepening structural inequality. Anthony Giddens (2000) suggests that contemporary globalization is the intensification of the process of modernity that began in Europe in the 1500s. Undoubtedly, the world economy is not the same as it was even just fifty years ago. There have been some fundamental changes, including the reduction of trade barriers, the acceleration of capital mobility, and the intensification of the global division of labor. George Ritzer defines globalization as "the worldwide diffusion of practices, expansion of relations across continents, organization of social life on a global scale, and growth of a shared global consciousness" (2004, 72). Some suggest that, due to these changes, the state is withering away. There is, however, no evidence to support any such weakening. Instead, the state's defined role is changing as it becomes more an instrument with which the global capitalist class can manage its assets within a particular society than an institution that responds to the demands of the people internal to that society.

Globalization per se is not a new development. It began when Europeans sailed to the New World. However, contemporary capitalism involves greater interconnectivity between the economic, political, and cultural/ideological dimensions than ever before, via markets, financial institutions, goods and services, and transnational corporate networks (Chase-Dunn 1999). How groups are incorporated into the process depends both on their overall position within the global distribution of power among nation-states and on their power position within their respective nation-states. The process of globalization is not linear; rather, it is fraught with contradictions. It embraces different rhythms of accumulation; it is more advanced in some sectors of society and the economy while lagging behind in others, even within the same country; and, while it increases wealth for some, it generates significant poverty for others. Globalization can be seen as having three levels: the suprastatal, the statal, and the intrastatal. Each level in turn has three dimensions—the economic, the political, and the cultural/ideological—all of which have a dialectical relationship with each other (Ramsaran and Price 2003).

Globalization is not only an economic phenomenon but also a cultural one. An important question then becomes, what is the impact of continued modernization on indigenous cultures? Some suggest that increased globalization leads to greater social and cultural homogeneity, while others suggest the opposite, that it leads to heterogeneity. This issue takes on greater significance within the context of the postcolonial state, which is subject to considerable external influence from more powerful social and political entities operating within the global economy. To construct a political entity, nation-states have attempted to create national identities. Anthony Smith defines a nation as "a named human population sharing an historic territory, common myths and historical memories, a mass public culture, a common economy and common legal rights and duties for all members" (1991, 14). Those regions of the world that underwent colonization were home to multiple racial/ethnic groups, with one racial group—in most instances, Europeans—dominant in the economic, political, and cultural spheres. During the decolonization process, one racial group or an alliance of several attempted to create a common national identity for nation-building purposes. Generally, however, forging that national culture led to the exclusion of some racial groups in the society.

Although it was colonialism that invented many of the racial and ethnic divisions in colonies, the process of globalization exacerbates these tensions and exploits differences for its own ends. Globalization may result in transnational identities, complex identities, or the "de-emphasis of ethnic identification in favor of broader alternative identities" (Anderson 2001, 216). However, globalization can also lead to a revival of ethnic identity in the face of mass culture and in defiance of any homogenizing tendency. Alan Anderson, drawing on Alberto Melucci (1989), suggests that

> a revival of ethnicity may prove to be a response to a need for collective identity. Thus, ethnicity is revived as a source of identity because it responds to a collective need that assumes a particular importance in complex societies. . . . As other criteria of group membership [such as class] weaken or recede, ethnic solidarity also responds to a need for identity of an eminently symbolic nature. (Anderson 2001, 217)

Dislocation resulting from globalization, then, can lead to a revival of traditional racial claims and identities. The disruption occasioned by the globalization process prompts groups to articulate their positions in ways specific to the local situation. Their reaction may be oriented toward race but can also address religion, gender, and class.

It is important to understand the contingent relationship that exists between the process of globalization and the question of race. Ambalavaner Sivanandan brings this relationship into sharp relief; looking at the relationship between racism, imperialism, and globalization, he notes that imperialism is the project, globalization the process, culture the vehicle, and the nation state the political and military agent.... To look at globalization without relating it to imperialism and therefore to racism is not only to regard its penetration into the Third World countries as an inevitable extension of trade and not a precursor to regime change that follows in its wake, but to overlook the racist discourse that accompanies it and in turn feeds into popular racism. (2005, 3)

Although we tend to see globalization purely in economic terms, embedded in that process is a historical relationship between appropriation and the capitalist ideology that is used to legitimize that appropriation; racist ideology plays a critical role in this process as well.

Race has an impact on globalization, and vice versa, not only in former colonial societies but also in countries lacking a colonial history. Walter Persaud (2005), looking at the changing structure of the US economy, has demonstrated that the restructuring has benefited those who control and manage capital, namely whites. He further demonstrates that poverty rates are higher in those states with a greater proportion of minorities. Also, looking at the impact of globalization in the United States, Andrew Barlow notes: "[T]he United States in particular is experiencing the most rapid growth of income inequality in the nation's history" (2003, 64). The financial collapse in 2008 has had a major impact along racial lines. Hope Yen, writing for the Associated Press in 2011, reported that the wealth gap between whites and nonwhites was the highest it had ever been since the 1970s: "The recession and uneven recovery have erased decades of minority gains, leaving whites on average with 20 times the net worth of blacks and 18 times that of Hispanics, according to an analysis of new Census data" (Yen 2011). While everyone else lost out in the recession, white wealth rebounded quickly. This crisis highlighted historical differences in wages. Joseph Stiglitz notes that "over the last three decades those with low wages (in the bottom 90 percent) have seen a growth of only around 15 percent in their wages, while those in the top 1 percent have seen an increase of almost 150 percent and the top 0.1 percent more than 300 percent" (2012, 8). With respect to wealth, he notes that "even after the great recession, the wealthiest 1 percent of households had 225 times the wealth of the typical American, almost double the ratio in 1962 or 1983" (2012, 8). Many have attributed the rise of Donald Trump to the negative impacts of globalization on the white working class, in particular the outsourcing of manufacturing jobs in the United States.

Furthermore, the decline of the welfare state (although not the decline of corporate welfare) has disproportionately affected minorities in the United States. Indeed, Eduardo Bonilla-Silva (2004) suggests that these changes in the US economy are resulting in a profound shift in the demographic structure of global society. Looking at Europe, he notes:

> The new world systemic need for capital accumulation has led to the incorporation of "dark" foreigners as "guest workers" and even as permanent workers.... Thus, today European nations have racial minorities in their midst who are progressively becoming more underclass.... [These nations] have developed an internal "racial structure" to maintain white power and have a curious racial ideology that combines ethnonationalism with a race-blind ideology similar to the colour-blind racism of the United States today. (Bonilla-Silva 2004, 935)

Thus, a changing racial hierarchy and a justifying ideology accompany the changing structure of the US economy. In Europe, this is seen in the resurgence of white nationalism, and in the case of Great Britain the "Brexit" move to delink from the European market.

In the case of Trinidad, the creolization process can result in increased homogeneity (i.e., Indo-Trinidadians assimilating into the dominant African creole forms of culture), increased heterogeneity (i.e., Indo-Trinidadians redefining their culture to separate themselves from the dominant African creole culture), or changes in some elements of the dominant African creole culture. In the latter case, African Trinidadian society becomes partially incorporated into Indo-Trinidadian creole culture. Racial identity in Trinidad remains a key variable around which both Indo- and African Trinidadians vie for state resources; however, that identity is not static, and the creolization process can provide important insights into how the process works in plural societies. Caribbean society largely evolves through mutual adjustments and reciprocal interactions among the major cultural sectors in the society. In the case of Trinidad, the foundation of racial identity was established in the colonial state with its race/class/color hierarchy. Racial groupings were defined within this framework vis-à-vis other groups in society, and power was an essential element with respect to how those positions evolved. Aisha Khan notes that Indo-Trinidadians define their racial identity "partly in relation to aspects of Afro-Trinidadian cultural characteristics, and partly in relation to aspects of their own cultural heritage" (2004, 15). Inevitably, there are elements of adjustment, mixing, and the reestablishment of separating markers.

In a society such as Trinidad's, where race has been a key organizing factor in the distribution of state power, it now becomes the principal arena where the negative effects of globalization are hashed out. Some have suggested that the impact of globalization can intensify the problems inherent to a system that uses race as an organizing principle. Furthermore, because political parties use clientelist strategies to reproduce state power and in turn distribute resources, race becomes an even more potent organizing principle whereby one's racial identity, in large measure, determines how one is treated in society. The contestation over material resources and cultural space in the public arena intensifies as the process of globalization deepens, and globalization's contradictions with respect to resource allocation become apparent. In the political arena, race is a defining principle with respect to how public policy is interpreted.

RACE AND PUBLIC POLICY

Ever since Trinidad inherited the Westminster (parliamentary) system of government in 1962, race has been one of the most important organizing principles in the contest for state power. The economic bases of Trinidadian and Tobagonian society are petroleum, heavy industry, and manufacturing. Historically, white Europeans controlled the political, economic, and social life of colonial Trinidad. After the

Second World War, a period of self-government ensued. The struggle for full statehood was articulated using the discourse of nationalism, which was framed primarily with African creole and European creole symbols, and almost no Indian creole symbols.

> The movement for self-determination involved the deployment of a particular cultural history, one that would legitimate the incipient vision of a nation, thereby providing the formula for homogeneous programs. In Trinidad the "discovery" and deployment of Creole lower-class patterns by the Creole middle class and upper classes took place at this historical juncture. Middle class artists looked to lower class Afro-Creole forms for local inspiration and politicians found these forms suitable cultural raw material for their nation building agenda. (Munasinghe 2001, 195)

Indeed, party politics emerged with race as one of the primary organizing principles. The People's National Movement (PNM) contested the elections of 1956 with a nationalist agenda that was premised on creole culture, appealing mainly to urban African Trinidadians with some additional support from Muslim and Presbyterian Indo-Trinidadians. Their opponents, the Democratic Labor Party (DLP), were mainly rurally based, Hindu Indo-Trinidadians. The PNM won the election and remained in power for thirty years, until the 1986 election.

Opposition to the PNM always involved political parties predominantly made up of Indo-Trinidadians or some combination of Indo-Trinidadians and factions of the African Trinidadian population that had broken away from the PNM. The National Alliance for Reconstruction (NAR) between 1986 and 1991, the United National Congress (UNC) and Democratic Action Congress (DAC) between 1995 and 2000, and the People's Partnership (PP) between 2010 and 2015 all replaced the PNM during those respective periods as the party in power.

The Indo-Trinidadian population is also defined by class differences. Class divisions led to a split within the UNC; Winston Dookeran led a breakaway faction of the party and formed the

Congress of the People (COP) in 2006. The leadership of the UNC interpreted this split as the abandonment of Indo-Trinidadians with rural roots by those persons of Indian descent who had obtained a more favorable class position. Basdeo Panday referred to those who had left the UNC to form the COP as "knife-and-fork Indians," inferring that they had become too uppity because of their improved class positions to associate with Indo-Trinidadians who were not as well off. In traditional Hindu celebrations and among the first Indian immigrants to Trinidad, meals were eaten with one's fingers and not with cutlery, which led to the knife and fork becoming symbolic of those in the upper classes. In a sense, Panday was accusing upwardly mobile Indo-Trinidadians of abandoning their race to participate in the dominant creole culture of which African Trinidadians were the most important part. There are other peculiarities of the Trinidad body politic that help explain its social and economic status.

Trinidad and Tobago has taken a more radical approach than most other Caribbean nations with respect to implementing the neoliberal development model proposed by the globalization project. Import substitution was not particularly successful; protected markets allowed local elites to make significant profits, but they did not transform society. The failure of import substitution, along with the advent of the Black Power movement, forced the state both to promote the People's Sector in the 1970s and to aggressively nationalize the country's primary natural resources, petroleum and sugar. The collapse of oil prices in the early 1980s exposed the structural weakness of the economy. A period of currency adjustments and a reduction in government spending did not solve the problems, ultimately resulting in the PNM's removal from power in 1986. The PNM had embraced the neoliberal model in the mid-1980s, and it was briefly the country's dominant ideology informing economic development until a change of government in 1986.

From 1988 to 1991, the NAR government implemented a full structural adjustment program with significant support from some of the most powerful elements of the business elite. The state's policy was to reduce the role of government in the economy, radically reform the civil service and public enterprises, significantly reform regulations so as to encourage direct foreign investment, and institute a process of rapid trade liberalization and privatization of state enterprises. The government's reduced role became most apparent in the areas of privatization and the government's allocation to direct employment. There were also significant changes in the area of trade liberalization. The import-licensing regime was replaced with a system of import tariffs. The economy was also opened up to direct foreign investment. By 2005, Trinidad was the second-largest recipient of direct foreign investment in the Caribbean, and more of the country's assets were owned by foreigners than by locals (*Trinidad Guardian* 2002). Additionally, a number of indirect taxes were removed while a value-added tax at the point of sale was introduced. By 1993, the government had completely liberalized the currency market, floating the rate of exchange. The liberalization process also accelerated in the real estate and financial sectors. The short-term impact of these policies was increased unemployment, inflation, and wage reduction; however, despite changes of government in 1991, 1995, 2001, and 2010, the policy direction remained consistent.

Between 2000 and 2006, the government announced that the country had experienced average annual GDP growth of 7.7 percent, with the economy doubling in size from US$51.4 billion to $101 billion. This growth was entirely due to the increase in petroleum prices globally. The PNM government resorted to a series of populist policies to address the issue of inequality, including increases in old-age pensions, the minimum wage, salaries for civil servants, spending on public housing, and spending on "make-work" schemes, to assist those who were the least financially stable in the society. The government also established some parastatal industries to oversee major government expenditures in public infrastructure. Many of these policies, however, were seen as an attempt to continue the failed policies of the 1970s and to use state funds as political largesse. The International Monetary Fund as early as 2007 warned the government that Trinidad was in danger of completely depleting all its savings by the year 2020 (the year the government had set to attain developed-country status) if it continued its rate of public spending. In 2008, however, the economy began to contract and experience negative growth. Accusations of extensive corruption in some of the major parastatal institutions resulted in the defeat of the PNM and the election of the PP in that year. Despite the changes of government throughout this period, and some minor adjustments in public policy initiatives, "there were no shifts between these administrations in the attitude and approach to the market as the prime mover of growth" (Farrell 2012b, 180). Although some aspects of racial identity receded into the background, when it came to the distribution of public resources, the racial lens remained the primary method for interpreting how development policies would impact the population. One specific example in which the issue of race was crucial in the determination of public policy involved the closure of Caroni Limited.

CARONI LIMITED

The PNM, returning to power in 2001, continued with its program of neoliberal development and divestment. Ever since the 1970s, the state-owned sugar company, Caroni Limited, had been a drain on the national treasury. The government sought to address this hemorrhage of resources by first closing down and then restructuring the company. The sugar sector employed predominately persons of Indian descent, which meant that most of the people who would be retrenched were Indo-Trinidadians. This move by the PNM government was interpreted invariably in racial terms. The leader of the opposition, Basdeo Panday, charged that the decision to close down Caroni Limited had nothing to do with economics but rather was due to racism and discrimination by the PNM government. He further suggested that the government's decision was based on the desire to break the political base of the UNC, which was rooted in the sugar industry. Addressing a crowd of supporters, he argued: "The regime has been able to treat you like dirt and with contempt and disrespect because they believe that you will not fight back, they think you are cowards, they regard you [as] docile cowards who will sell out your fellow victims for a CEPEP contract and an invitation to a cocktail party" (*Trinidad Express* 2005c). Indeed, Mr. Panday was evoking the traditional stereotype that had been held by the colonial British and creole middle class that Indo-Trinidadians were docile and easily controlled.

There was also the perception that the government's concern about economic viability was peculiarly limited, because although the government claimed to have closed Caroni Limited for economic reasons, it was simultaneously developing public works schemes through CEPEP[1] that were not economically profitable but that benefited the PNM's African Trinidadian supporters. A letter to the editor of the *Trinidad Express* made the argument this way: "While the PNM closes down Caroni with a brutal neglect for the livelihood of over 30,000 citizens affected, we read of the massive corruption in the CEPEP program where they literally give away money to party hacks and their relatives to cut grass on the roadways (*Trinidad Express* 2005b). In another letter published by the *Trinidad Guardian* on January 26, 2007, Stephen Kangal wrote:

> The princely sum of $1.6 billion was spent to keep 4,000 CEPEP people wastefully engaged in non-productive employment. When the URP's criminally funded war-chest is added to CEPEP it would turn out to be a $2.5 billion bonanza. That windfall was neither subject to accountability nor transparency.... But the PNM Government found it a drain on the Treasury to dispense an annual subvention of $200 million to state-owned Caroni Ltd to keep 10,000, albeit a natural UNC constituency, to quote Danny Montano [a former minister of the PNM government], in productive employment.... All this dictatorial nonsense, squandermania and double standards are taking place while the protagonists of justice, fair-play and caring governance maintain their loud silence because one ethnic group is immediately benefiting and another docile one has been brought to their knees by an arrogant and spiteful regime. (*Trinidad Guardian* 2007)

Despite the change of government in 2010 with the emergence of the PP, race remained the lens through which both Indo- and African Trinidadians viewed the government's allocation of public works resources. The PP government did not seek to revive Caroni Limited but rather sought to increase the rate at which it compensated the failed enterprise's retrenched workers. A combination of land and money was promised to these workers by the PNM government.

CONTESTING RESOURCE DISTRIBUTION

Race continued to be central in the debate over access to the country's resources. Discontent against the UNC, as against the PNM, was articulated along racial lines. A popular calypsonian, Cro Cro (Weston Rawlins), in his calypso "Blackman (Dey) Look Fuh Dat" chastised African Trinidadians for not voting for the PNM, thus allowing the UNC to take control of the state. Under the UNC, which was perceived as an "Indian government," opponents made many allegations of corruption. Referring to the earlier arguments of the 1980s that Indo-Trinidadians controlled the private sector and African Trinidadians the state and the public sector, some people felt that Indo-Trinidadians now controlled both the private and public sectors and that the UNC government was allowing the Indian business sector to rob the country of its resources. Many felt that corruption was the cause of cost overruns in building a new international airport in the late 1990s, and in many other state projects. The resulting probe and subsequent charges laid against a group of businessmen who were involved in the airport project found that not only Indo-Trinidadian businessmen but also people of Chinese, mixed, and African descent were guilty. The scapegoat for public disdain, however, was Ishwar Galbaransingh, a businessman of Indian descent. Despite the various backgrounds of the persons charged, there was little discussion about whether Trinidad's business elite as a whole was involved in corrupt practices. Apart from businesspeople, former prime minister Basdeo Panday and his wife were charged and convicted for not complying with the Integrity Act by not declaring a substantial sum of money they held in a British bank account.

Even while the PNM was in power, many of the party's natural constituents, namely people employed in the public sector, also articulated their discontent along racial lines. However, when people of African descent voiced dissatisfaction with the PNM, they did not critique fellow African Trinidadians in the government, given that the PNM was perceived to represent their own interests, but rather the Syrian Trinidadian community, many of whom were key players among the economic elite and prominent members of the PNM cabinet. Jennifer Baptiste-Primus, then president general of the Public Servants Union (PSA), unleashed an attack on the Syrian Trinidadian community at a Labor Day rally speech in 2005, accusing persons of Syrian descent of thinking they controlled Trinidad and urging the population to "take back their country." In an Emancipation Day message to union members printed in the *Trinidad Express* on August 2, 2005, Baptiste-Primus continued her argument:

> Some describe them [Syrians] as entrepreneurs, as businessmen and/ or as capitalists. Others recognize them as unconscionable plunderers of the national patrimony avariciously consuming the societal economic pie giving no quarter to those who legitimately strive to seek out an existence on the discarded crumbs. . . . We must, without reservation defrock those who sanctimoniously shroud themselves in the apparel of upstanding nationals, honorable patriots and national builders. We must be real for all to see, the hypocrites, bloodsuckers, drug dealers and gun runners who have built and continue to build their evil empires, amassing phenomenal wealth at the expense of the lives and blood of the little black boys from Morvant, Laventille, and the Beetham.[2] (*Trinidad Express* 2005a)

Some prominent members of the Syrian Trinidadian community went on the offensive, condemning the statement and calling on Baptiste-Primus to withdraw it. They also called on other racial groups to rally support for their cause. They only found limited support, however; indeed, some argued that when the state had discriminated against other groups, especially Indo-Trinidadians, in the past, the Syrian Trinidadian community had not lent any solidarity. Although an economic powerhouse in Trinidadian society, the Syrian Trinidadian community is small in terms of numbers for electoral purposes and therefore incapable of rallying public support to defend against perceived racial injustice.

When the PP took control of the government in 2010, the new leaders promised openness, transparency, and accountability. They also promised to use the abundant resources accrued to the state from petroleum to enhance the lives of all the people of the country. As part of that promise, they proposed to decentralize the government by moving some of the major public ministries out of the capital city, Port of Spain, and relocating them to different parts of the country. This proposal was in response to massive traffic congestion issues around Port of Spain that had resulted from centralization. The proposal was also interpreted in racial terms. Keith Rowley, the PNM's leader and, at the time, leader of the opposition, accused the government of emptying out Port of Spain, which is populated primarily by African Trinidadians. He suggested that the relocation of these administrative offices to Chaguanas, a town in central Trinidad, was intended primarily to benefit the Indo-Trinidadians who lived there and who owned most of the town's businesses.

CRIME AND KIDNAPPING

Crime, particularly kidnapping, is another issue that has been interpreted in racial terms. From a theoretical perspective, increased crime is usually correlated with economic decline. In Trinidad and Tobago, violent crime is on the rise, particularly kidnapping for ransom. Such kidnappings are viewed not only as a law-and-order issue or an issue related to the collapse of civil society, but also as a racial issue. Many Indo-Trinidadian commentators in the popular press have argued that an overwhelming majority of people who have been kidnapped have been businesspeople of Indian descent, suggesting a deliberate targeting of the Indian population by African Trinidadian criminals. One prominent Indo-Trinidadian lawyer, Anand Ramlogan, argued in the *Trinidad Guardian* of September 25, 2005, that when Indians were kidnapped, the government did nothing, whereas when prominent members of the "Port of Spain elite" (namely, whites and Syrians) were targeted, the government took action. He also noted the widespread anxiety among Indo-Trinidadians on account of their being the special targets of kidnappings for ransom. Ramlogan continued:

The nation's worry is intensified by the fact that prior to the general election, the wave of kidnappings had suddenly stopped after the "truce" had been publicly-declared and signed by the "local community leaders." . . . A lot of people are beginning to wonder if, instead of the 13 Indians kidnapped thus far, it were 13 non-Indians residing in upper-class North Trinidad, where the government's response of "Hold strain"; we working on it man would have been the same. Somehow I doubt it. The Chamber has finally called on Government to seek foreign assistance. This, after the kidnapping of Justin Raymond-Guillen and Health Minister John Raheal's nephew, Dr. Eddie Koury. . . . The Port of Spain elite have been rocked by these kidnappings. They realize they are no longer safe or immune. MP Nizam Baksh's son was kidnapped and brutally murdered. Little Vijay Persad has never been found. The list of Indian businessmen kidnapped just keeps growing, but the Port of Spain business community pandered to the Government. No one from the Chamber saw the need for foreign intervention then. Truth be told, the Indian community is quietly thanking God for answering prayers. Their cries and pleas for help had simply gone unanswered for too long. The indifference and casual attitude of the authorities and the Port of Spain elite made them feel as if they were not part of the society. (*Trinidad Guardian* 2005)

Ramlogan became Trinidad's attorney general when the PP took over the government in 2010. Indeed, the PP argued that crime had become a major drawback to economic development, and therefore party leaders made crime reduction a central part of their political platform. They proposed, as a solution, to declare a state of emergency in August 2011 and implement a dawn-to-dusk curfew in places they designated "hot spots for crime." These designated areas were mainly urban areas where mostly poor African Trinidadians lived. Some African Trinidadian leaders saw this policy as a way for an aggressive Hindu attorney general, a white Canadian police commissioner, and an Indo-Trinidadian-dominated government to arrest hundreds of young African men. The strategy, however, did not have much success, since crime remains high even today, eight years later. Daily murders and drug-related offenses remain prominent features of life in Trinidad, and because many of the shootings are seen as gang related and occur in areas that are predominantly populated by people of African descent, race becomes part of the equation through which many Indo-Trinidadians come to understand the issue. "Little Black Boys," as they are called by Gypsy (Winston Peters) in a calypso, are now perceived as a major cause of crime and violence in Trinidadian society (Ryan 2013). The crime problem in Trinidad has intensified over the years, and neither the PNM nor the PP governments have had much success in stifling it.

CARICOM SINGLE MARKET AND ECONOMY

One of the provisions of the Caribbean Community's Single Market and Economy (CSME) allows for the free movement of skilled labor throughout the common market. It was introduced by Trinidad's PNM government in 2002 following an amendment to the Treaty of Chaguaramas, which established the community, known as Caricom. This provision, too, was interpreted in terms of race. People of Indian descent have frequently accused the PNM, particularly in the late 1960s and 1970s, of allowing Grenadian citizens to live in Trinidad in order to bolster their political support. It should be noted, however, that there has been a long history of migration to Trinidad and Tobago from other islands of the Caribbean, particularly Saint Lucia, Saint Vincent, and Barbados as well as Grenada. Many Indians viewed this movement of people from other Caricom countries, who are predominantly of African descent, as an attempt by the PNM government to bring in immigrants and locate them in marginal constituencies in order to pad the voting list and thus ensure PNM victories in elections. In a letter to the *Trinidad Express*, L. Rampersad argued:

By the importation of Caricom people into our country we may be importing thousands of criminals with the obvious expertise to get certain jobs done. This means that the lives of our citizens may be at stake as statistics relating to crime continue to reflect horror and concern. But what would be worse is having to accommodate such individuals in the most peaceful areas of lovely Trinbago such as Caroni and Penal (predominantly Indo Trinidadian occupied areas). An oil windfall that may result from America's war with Iraq will certainly be short lived. If we do embark on an importation of Caricom skilled individuals, our citizens will surely suffer from this action in the not too distant future. (*Trinidad Express* 2005b)

The migration of Caricom nationals into Trinidad and Tobago continues to be a hotly contested issue. And, conversely, when the PP government was in power, they were likewise accused of giving preference to the immigration of Guyanese nationals of Indian descent in order to increase their own political base.

RADIO LICENSE TO THE MAHA SABHA

Race is also an important tool for contesting public space in the face of a dominant culture. In a period of continuing modernization, groups who perceive themselves as marginalized escalate their contestation for space in the public culture. The process of creolization can sometimes allow a marginal group to contest the dominant culture and change it. The Indo-Trinidadian population has long seen itself as marginalized in Trinidad's "national culture." This is evident in the ethnic contestation that took place over the denial of a radio license to the Maha Sabha, the largest Hindu organization in Trinidad. The group applied for a license to operate a radio station in 2000. At the time, the UNC government was granting licenses to many other radio entrepreneurs. Winston Ragbir, the director of telecommunications, recommended to the cabinet that a radio license be granted to the Maha Sabha. However, when the PNM assumed power in 2001, the cabinet refused to grant the license without indicating why the request was denied. At the same time, Citadel Limited, which operated a number of radio stations and was run by a well-known PNM activist, Louis Lee Sing (later the mayor of Port of Spain), got a similar request approved. A falling out between Lee Sing and a business partner had resulted in one of Citadel's radio frequencies being taken out of service. Lee Sing, using his connections in government, quickly and easily got a new license approved. The Maha Sabha took their grievance to the courts, charging discrimination and citing the preferential treatment given to Citadel Limited. A court in Trinidad ruled that the cabinet had discriminated against the Maha Sabha but did not order the cabinet to grant the license, so the cabinet took no action. The matter then went to the Privy Council, which ruled that the Maha Sabha must be given a license. An editorial in the *Trinidad Express* of July 7, 2006, made the following comment:

> It is simply scandalous that the Privy Council was able to find a letter from the Permanent Secretary in the Ministry of Public Administration giving the reasons why an application for a radio license for the Maha Sabha's Central Broadcasting Systems Limited (CBSL) was never communicated to the applicants until after the matter was determined by the High Court. Questions also arise as to the basis on which the recommendations given by the then Director of Telecommunications for a license to be granted to CBSL was not accepted by the Cabinet. That recommendation had been made in 2000, well before the Cabinet received and approved a radio license for Citadel Limited, the radio company owned and managed by Louis Lee Sing, a high profile supporter of the ruling People's National Movement. . . . What all of this clearly points to is a pattern of developments which has the effect of perpetuating discrimination of immense proportions upon the Maha Sabha and the citizens for whom it speaks. The Attorney General, the Minister of Public Administration, and indeed the owners of Citadel Limited clearly have a case to answer as to why the country was made to suffer such indignities associated with this affair. Unbridled and unjustified favoritism has been at work here, to the detriment of Trinidad and Tobago's image as a country that aspires to provide an equal place for every creed and race.

Trinidad and Tobago Newsday (July 6, 2006) opined on the matter in a slightly different way:

So the Maha Sabha turned to the courts. And it was here that insult was added to injury. The High Court ruled in favor of the Maha Sabha but, instead of accepting this judgment, the AG decided to appeal. And when the Appeal Court upheld the decision, the AG still did not back down, but went all the way to the Privy Council—a decision that would now cost the taxpayers several million dollars, since the Law Lords, quite rightly, ordered that the State pay the appellant's cost. But the question remains as to why the AG and the Government took this issue so far. If the AG has a reasonable explanation, the public must hear it. If such an explanation is not forthcoming, citizens will assume that only bias could have informed the AG's strategy—and since the appellant in this case is the largest Hindu organization in Trinidad and Tobago, the bias inferred is an especially unpleasant kind.

Despite the ruling, there was much delay in granting the license; eventually, the Maha Sabha began calling for the attorney general to be charged with contempt of court, after which the license was granted. The lawyer who took the Maha Sabha's case was Anand Ramlogan, who was also involved in a case discussed above. This situation was articulated in the public arena as an African Trinidadian government deliberately discriminating against Hindus and Indo-Trinidadians.

THE TRINITY CROSS DISPUTE

The Trinity Cross, awarded for distinguished service to the country, is Trinidad's highest honor. For years, non-Christian Indo-Trinidadians frequently complained that the award was discriminatory. Indeed, some Hindu recipients even refused to accept the award. The Maha Sabha and the Islamic Relief Center filed a suit in June 2005 in the courts arguing that the award discriminated against Hindus and Muslims. Although Justice Peter Jamadar ruled that the award indeed discriminated as charged, the court went on to rule that, because its power was limited to settling law in Trinidad and Tobago, it couldn't force the state to withdraw the award. The government, then under Prime Minister Patrick Manning, agreed with the court's ruling and decided to appoint a committee to look into an appropriate award for distinguished service to replace the Trinity Cross.

Reactions to these events were often guided by racial identity. Mellitus Barnes, in a June 13, 2006, letter to the *Trinidad Guardian*, noted:

> In a nation where there are so many Christian churches and a born again Christian Prime Minister, we have allowed non-Christians to dictate to us. Surely we have failed the test. . . . Christ died for all. There is no discrimination. People of all ethnic groups have access to his grace. He is the only prophet who died and was resurrected. Prophets from other religious persuasions have died and remained dead. (*Trinidad Guardian* 2006b)

The most eloquent and damning response came from a popular calypsonian, Hollis Liverpool (the Mighty Chalkdust). In an open letter to Prime Minister Manning printed in the *Trinidad Express* on June 13, 2006, Liverpool argued that Justice Jamadar had erred. He said that a case could be made for considering the sociological and cultural context within which the Trinity Cross award had been established. Given the award's cultural background, Liverpool claimed that it was national in significance and not religious, even thought the name of the award carried religious resonance.

> One cannot take the history of thousands of Christians who have laboured in the vineyard for centuries and throw it all down into the abyss of forgetfulness and despair in one fell swoop, simply because one of the Christian traditions appears unfriendly to a non-Christian. To do so is to show total disrespect for history, the numerous dead and the tens of thousands who have given their all to Trinidad and Tobago. Moreover, it is total disrespect for all the Trinbagonian Christians who are not yet born, and who because of the wiles of a few mischievous and attention-grabbing persons may never hear of or understand fully, the holy, viable and extant traditions of their ancestors. This is not politics, Mr. Manning; this is culture; this is life. It was Aristotle, speaking on democracy, who said: "One principle of liberty is for all to rule and be ruled in turn, and indeed democratic

justice is the application of numerical not proportionate equality." It was Abraham Lincoln who intoned: "You cannot help the poor by overtaxing the rich." Paradoxically, you cannot help the non-Christians by trampling upon the traditions of the Christians. History, Mr. Manning, will condemn you.

In 2008, the name of the award was changed to the Order of the Republic of Trinidad and Tobago. However, Trinidadians continue to make similar challenges with respect to how much state funding is given to specific Christian or non-Christian festivals in Trinidad as well as the amount of funding provided to "Indian" or "non-Indian" cultural projects.

CONTESTATION FOR PUBLIC SERVICE JOBS

With increased Indo-Trinidadian participation in education came increased competition for jobs in the public sector, an area long perceived to be the domain of African Trinidadians. This issue came to the fore with respect to recruitment and promotion in the Police Service. Anand Ramlogan was once again at the center of the controversy. He took a case to court in which he argued that members of the Police Service were being passed over for promotion into the senior ranks because of their race. He took issue with one newspaper article that suggested that not many Indo-Trinidadians were applying to join the police, writing:

> The argument that Indians don't apply in equal numbers for jobs in the public service is incorrect. This is a thing of the colonial past. In the past 50 years that has not been the case. Where are the statistics and evidence to back up this claim I ask? The fear and reluctance of compiling racial statistics shall forever force us to argue on emotional perceptions without reference to facts. Even so, doesn't it beg the question: Why are they not applying? Is it because they feel there is inequality in promotion and career advancement? "Dey doh apply" is a trite excuse that is no longer accepted in modern coun-

tries because it is in itself symptomatic of a racially unequal system. (*Trinidad Guardian* 2006a)

The perception that one political party uses its state power to distribute largesse to individuals with the race typically associated with that party has continued with the PP government. Two appointments to prominent positions in public service again brought the racial issue to the forefront. Prime Minister Kamla Persad-Bissessar announced that the Security Intelligence Agency (SIA) had been directed by her predecessor, Patrick Manning, to spy on her and wiretap her conversations. After the dust settled on this fiasco, Persad-Bissessar removed the incumbent head of the SIA, a person of African Trinidadian descent, and appointed Trevor Ganpat, an Indo-Trinidadian who was an experienced security analyst, to replace him. But then Ganpat's appointment was revoked without explanation, and Reshmi Ramnarine, an Indo-Trinidadian woman with very limited qualifications and negligible experience in the field, was appointed to head the agency. After public outcry, Ramnarine's appointment was also revoked, again without adequate public explanation.

Another appointment to raise concern was that of the governor of the Central Bank. When the outgoing governor's term ended in July 2012, the Persad-Bissessar administration appointed a forty-four-year old economist, Jwala Rambarran, to the post. In both instances, race became the bone of contention. Terrence Farrell, a former deputy governor of the Central Bank, wrote a letter to the *Trinidad Express* entitled "No Sacred Cows" to voice his displeasure at the selection process. He argued that the process should have been transparent and that there were suitably qualified candidates of African Trinidadian descent whom the government ignored.

> In my estimation, the Bank had at least three very good internal candidates. Shelton Nicholls has been Deputy Governor for ten years, having worked in the Bank before as an economist. He holds degrees in Economics from UWI and his PhD is from the University of London. He is one of the finest quantitative economists in the region with several academic publications, and now has ten years of policy-

making experience under his belt. He came from humble beginnings in Tobago, is fluent in French and a man of considerable artistic ability besides. Alvin Hilaire, the Bank's chief economist, obtained First Class Honours in Economics at UWI and holds a PhD from Columbia University. He worked as an economist at the Bank and then pursued a career at the International Monetary Fund which included several missions and a stint as Resident Representative in Guinea, Africa. He is fluent in French. Hilaire grew up from humble beginnings in East Port of Spain. Joan John, the current Deputy Governor, Operations has a career in the Bank of over 30 years, has worked as an economist and has run the Foreign Exchange and Banking Operations departments. She has been instrumental in modernising the country's payments systems. She is from Laventille. (Farrell 2012a)

Farrell lumped the Ramnarine and Rambarran appointments in the same category. He suggested that the Persad-Bissessar government had an agenda to get people of its kind, namely those of Indian descent, in all the key institutions of the state.

This latest appointment, which comes up well short of appropriateness, will I think not be the last such that we will see. Reshmi Ramnarine's appointment was characterized as a "misstep," but the succession of similar appointments at key institutions suggests otherwise. It suggests that there is an agenda afoot. I am advised that State enterprise directors at an orientation meeting held at National Academy for the Performing Arts were told that the important quality of a director was "loyalty." Directors must indeed be loyal, to their companies, to the rule of law, to integrity and to their consciences. I suspect though that the loyalty required is political, and blind loyalty to partisan political agendas could lead to the compromising of integrity, and worse. The next big target will be the appointment of the President of the Republic. I do not think that anyone took seriously the Prime Minister's suggestion that a third term could be on offer to President Max Richards. In any event I rather doubt that he would be open to it. The appointment of the President unlocks the door to other appointments—judges, chairmen and members of service commissions and "independent" senators—and will mute any criticism on the misuse of the country's defense force against civil society. These positions are critical given that some as yet unknown proposals for constitutional reform will emerge in the next year. (Farrell 2012a)

When President Richards stepped down in 2013, the PP government appointed a prominent high court judge of mixed African Trinidadian descent to replace him. And in December 2015, after the PNM returned to power, Rambarran's appointment was revoked and Alvin Hilaire was appointed as the new governor of the Central Bank. Once more, prestigious and lucrative appointments in the public sector were interpreted along lines of race.

Throughout this chapter, we have attempted to show how racial identity can be an important factor in the way public policy is interpreted. We have also sought to show how one of the inherent contradictions of contemporary modernity, increased output existing alongside increasing social inequality, can be interpreted along racial lines. These factors are even more prominent in a postcolonial society where race is the major organizing principle around which political parties operate. They demonstrate how economic issues, when distorted behind the smokescreen of race, can pose serious obstacles to societal transformation. As long as the political structures reinforce racial solidarity, nation building will remain a difficult prospect. Initial attempts to build a nation state in a postcolonial environment often mobilize the population around a blend of nationalisms, which in the Caribbean can be a combination of European and African creole cultures. In some ways, this tendency further entrenches the racial divide that colonialism first produced. In Trinidad, the divide has not developed into open and violent racial hostility as in other societies where similar circumstances prevail. The reason might be attributed to the creolization process, in which two major racial groups begin to share some common cultural practices in their own way. The creolization process, however, is contradictory. On the one hand, the two major racial groups may become somewhat more homogeneous in some cultural practices, but on the other, the political process, organized along racial lines and in conjunction with the clientelist tendencies of the postcolonial state, attempts to divide racial groups and reestablish racial solidarity. As the calypsonian David Rudder notes in his 2003 calypso "Trini to de Bone": "How we vote is not how we party."

Moreover, as the modernization process deepens, the Indo-Trinidadian community competes for ever more space in the public culture, consistently articulating its identity in opposition to African Trinidadian identity. Indeed, what we are witnessing is an attempt to rewrite the national culture, which was/is essentially based on the African creole experience, to include with equal weight what Indo-Trinidadians consider their contribution to Trinidadian society. That Indo-Trinidadian culture is changing the dominant culture also suggests that other groups are going to be changing, either contesting or adopting elements of the dominant culture. On many fronts, Indo-Trinidadian influence has grown apace, and the "Ganges has met the Nile," as evidenced in soca, chutney, carnival, Phagwah, and many other artistic media. However, in the political sphere, where binding decisions are routinely made regarding the distribution of resources, cultural rewriting remains highly underdeveloped. The fluidity of this process is evident in the rise and fall of Jack Warner within the political ranks of the UNC. Warner, a businessman, emerged as an African Trinidadian voice in the UNC in the late 1990s; Basdeo Panday had originally brought him into the party. Although other African Trinidadian politicians have been active in the UNC in the past, they exercised power only insofar as the party leadership allowed. Warner, however, developed a strong political base among a predominately Indo-Trinidadian constituency in Chaguanas. Indeed, he was instrumental in ousting Panday, the party's traditional patriarch, and installing Persad-Bissessar as party leader. Warner was elected in a borough, Chaguanas, that is considered the heartland of the UNC and where the majority of the constituents are Indo-Trinidadians. He subsequently split from the UNC and formed his own political party, the Independent Liberal Party, and in a by-election was able to defeat the UNC candidate in Chaguanas. He was embraced by the predominantly Indo-Trinidadian electorate in his district, and many elements in the UNC, now his opponents, sought to highlight his African Trinidadian roots. At the height of the campaign for the by-election, Prime Minister Persad-Bissessar referred to him as a "lagahoo" (a mythical shape-shifting monster). By the 2015 general election, however, the Indo-Trinidadian population had returned to its "natural" political base, and Warner's party lost in nationwide voting.

The process of creolization, then, modulates how race relations develop in the context of modernization and the neoliberal agenda. Whereas in some aspects the creolization process makes two distinct groups more alike, in others—particularly in the political arena—their differences are reinforced. In the continuing process of moderniza-tion—specifically with respect to economic developments—racial differences will continue to be highlighted as long as the contestation for state power and the organization of political parties remain based on the colonial experience. But perhaps the process of creolization can begin to transform the political system away from its racial axis toward a more class-based system that can better address the issues of inequality and modernization.

Hindu temple by the sea, Waterloo, Trinidad. Photo by Sherry Dubarry.

Jhandi celebration at a Hindu temple, Waterloo, Trinidad. Photo by Sherry Dubarry.

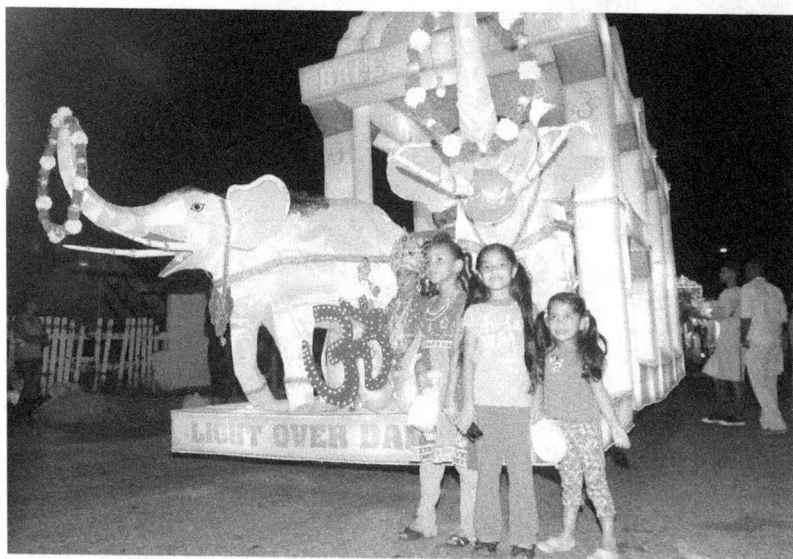

Diwali celebration, Guyana. Courtesy of Stabroek News.

Samdaye Sonny, Trinidad. Reprinted with permission of Andrea de Silva.

Phagwah celebration, Guyana. Courtesy of Stabroek News.

Phagwah celebration, Guyana. Courtesy of Stabroek News.

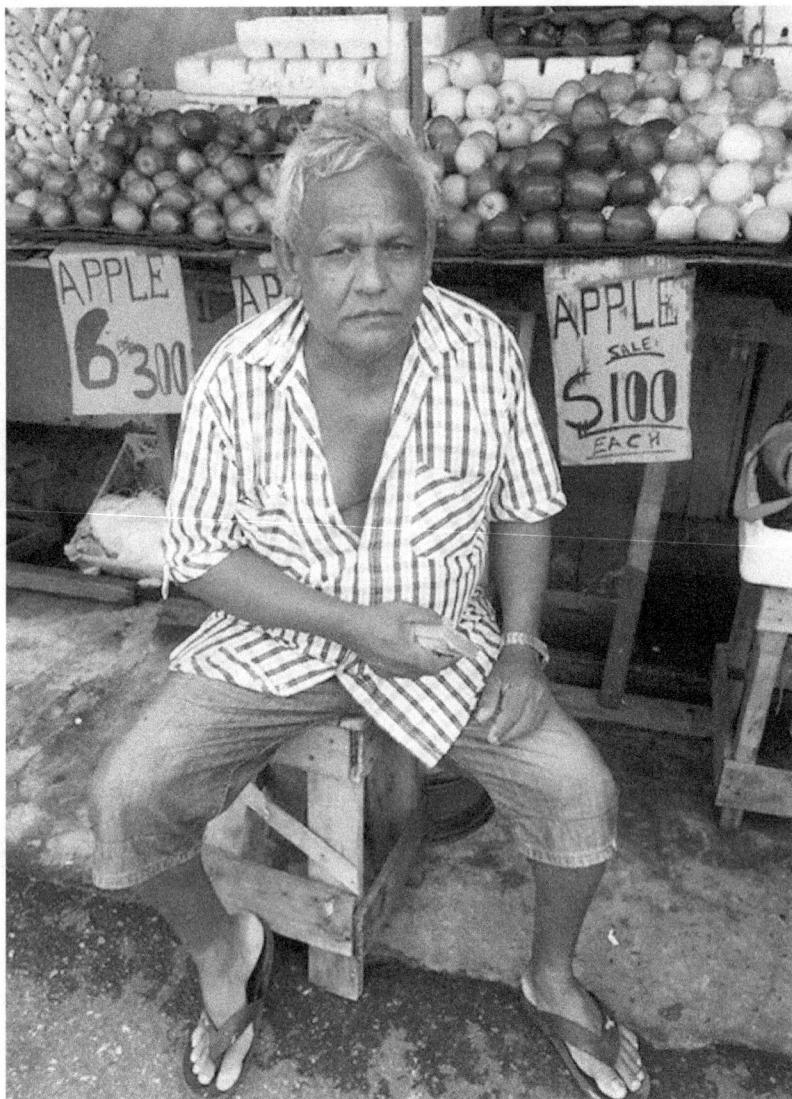

Narine Beharry. Photo by Linden Lewis.

Tassa drummers, South Oropouche, Trinidad. Photo by Sherry Dubarry.

Hindu cremation ceremony. Photo by Sherry Dubarry.

3

"Dig Dutty"

The Practice of Matikor among Hindus in Guyana and Trinidad

The notion of ritual in certain areas of life in the Caribbean is conceived of in one of two ways. First is the exotic, conjuring ideas of strangeness involving animal sacrifices, superstitions, spirit possession, and other practices more akin to magic and obeah (necromancy). Second is through the discourse of denial. Often defining their rituals in a religious or anthropological sense, Caribbean people insist that the region has no real rituals associated with fertility, circumcision, funerals, childbirth, or specific rites of passage. The notion of ritual is often reduced to sacrifice within the context of some of the indigenous religions of the Caribbean, namely Shango, Vodou, and Santería, or more explicitly in obeah procedures and in the practice of Kali-Mai Puja,[1] of which more will be said subsequently. The observance of ritual in the consciousness of everyday life is hardly considered or rarely acknowledged. The practice of going to church every Sunday or Saturday, hosting a wake or "nine-nights" ceremony following a death, or visiting the gravesite of a deceased relative does not always register as ritual in the popular consciousness in the Caribbean, but most such actions clearly fall into that category.

A ritual refers to specifically repeated forms of observable behavior that are often symbolic and that operate in a specific universe of meanings. Adam Seligman and colleagues note that ritual provides "an orientation to action and hence a framing of action that is relevant in understanding human activities beyond what may be done in temples, churches, mosques—or the houses of Parliament for [that] matter" (2008, 5). As Mary Douglas notes, ritual helps us to select certain experiences for concentrated attention (2002, 78). This broader framing of action is at the center of this chapter on the Matikor or "Dig Dutty" ritual in Guyana and Trinidad;[2] it provides direction for collective cultural memory and connects the past to the present (Douglas 2002, 79). Rituals are always sites of meaning and understanding and are often performed in accordance with various objectives. In addition to the immediate objective of the activity, rituals usually serve a specific sociological function for society, as Émile Durkheim so eloquently pointed out in *The Elementary Forms of Religious Life* (1995).

In his iconic last work, Durkheim focused on religion and ritual insofar as they establish social norms, which produce and reproduce meaning in everyday life. It is through rituals, according to Durkheim (1995), that a group becomes conscious of itself as a group. While we believe that other factors such as social class, race, gender, and nationalism preponderate in the formation of group identity and solidarity, we nevertheless understand his point about the importance of ritual to the collective consciousness. For him, a group operating collectively in a symbolic universe is largely responsible for producing group cohesion and group solidarity. In other words, for Durkheim, ritual is supremely social and provides us with considerable insight into understanding society. Rituals are performances, public or private, that reinforce or modify culture. In many ways, rituals represent the values of some groups; "they convey meaning to audiences, although ritual organizers and participants seldom think about the meaning and implications of these rituals" (Magolda 2003, 780). All rituals involve a performance, an audience of some sort, distinct roles, and symbols. Rituals can also change over time depending on the context in which they are performed.

Furthermore, they can be used as a sort of public signifier to separate those who practice the ritual from those who don't.

The Matikor/Dig Dutty ritual is both public and personal. It is public in that it includes a performative aspect, but it is also personal in that at least part of the ritual is enacted on the body. In this chapter, then, we aim not so much to use the Matikor/Dig Dutty ritual to understand wider Guyanese or Trinidadian society as to gain some insight into the cultural meaning associated with one aspect of Hindu religious practice. We will explore the ritual significance of the Matikor/Dig Dutty ritual in order to examine its social function and the part it plays in developing and reproducing religious and cultural meaning, and to contextualize its persistence.

Although Matikor/Dig Dutty has often been viewed as a ritual performed by women—and it certainly seemed to have had that kind of exclusivity initially—it has been modified in recent years to involve men. Despite this change, however, many still view the ritual as a space for women. When asked if he participated in the Dig Dutty ritual in Guyana, a young Indo-Guyanese taxi driver responded: "That is really a lady's thing, you know." The Matikor/Dig Dutty ritual as a place of special social and political significance is captured in the following observation by Rosanne Kanhai (1999, ix):

> Matikor was a place of healing where women could act out their resistance against the degradation and depersonalization imposed upon them by the ruling class. As a grassroots Hindu festival, communal religious rituals were embedded in matikor activities, thus bringing together the sacred and the profane, the carnal and the spiritual, the political and the social. (1999, xi)

Kanhai goes on to argue that "as Indian women enter into Caribbean and global mainstreams, matikor acts as a reminder of the spiritual strength found in community and tradition" (1999, ix). Women's rituals have taken on particular significance; some have argued that they allow women to resist society's patriarchal arrangements. To characterize all such acts as resistance, however, would be too simplistic:

Scholars of women and religion in many contexts have observed that women tend to reinterpret or reconfigure predominant religious practices and ideologies in ways that reflect women's specific values and experiences. To refer to most, or all of such reconfigurations, as "resistance," is to dilute significantly the meaning of that term. Issues of gender hegemony, furthermore, including questions of compliance with and resistance to male authority and hegemonic structures and codes are rarely straightforward. (Pintchman 2004, 23)

Hindu women are traditionally viewed as being somewhat confined within the family. Their position in society might best be understood in terms of how the Hindu family in the Caribbean has functioned. Indians came to the Caribbean as indentured workers after emancipation in 1838. One of the most noticeable features of Indian communities during this early period was the shortage of women. Morton Klass (1961), looking at Trinidad, noted that the Indo-Trinidadian family was essentially a patriarchal, extended family that was closely governed by rules and regulations. Parents arranged their children's marriages, for example. Initially, children had no veto rights, although in later years betrothed couples were introduced to each other prior to marriage. Most men were considered to be of marriageable age between sixteen and thirty years old, whereas women were only eligible between the ages of fifteen and eighteen. If a woman were not married by age eighteen, it was considered an embarrassment to her family. It was often feared that she would be in danger of losing her virginity and getting pregnant, or worse, getting involved with a man of African descent, liaisons that some believed would pollute the race. Generally, Indians believed that women had to be closely monitored, since they were presumed not to have the ability to resist sexual advances.

In Guyana as in Trinidad, the pressures of a multicultural society made it difficult for the Indo-Trinidadian community to reproduce the family forms of traditional India. One factor that contributed to the changing role of the Indo-Trinidadian woman was access to education. Until 1946, about 65 percent of Indo-Trinidadian women over the age of ten were illiterate (Mohammed 1988, 389). Increased state spending on education in the postindependence period, the introduction of a common entrance examination for secondary high school (which offered the perception of equal opportunities for both males and females to education), and the practical necessity for education with the changing nature of the economy all contributed to the weakening of Indo-Trinidadian patriarchy. The changes that occurred in Trinidad were largely replicated in Guyana, where Indian women followed a similar trajectory in terms of both accessing education and asserting greater autonomy.

The opening up of the economy in the 1960s and 1970s also resulted in changes to the Indo-Trinidadian family and the role of women. As the economy began to grow, more educational opportunities became available and spaces were created in the public sector where women could gain employment (Mohammed 1988, 391). Indeed, the Indo-Trinidadian family, like its counterpart in Guyana, began to move away from the extended family into a more nuclear family structure. However, men have continued to retain, at least to some degree, responsibility for decision making, greater freedom of mobility than women enjoy, and the ability to exercise power in the family. Moreover, even though many Indian women are employed outside the home, caregiving continues to be an important female function. It is in this context that one must interpret how the Matikor/Dig Dutty ritual is changing with respect to Hindu identity vis-à-vis that of other sectors of society and its impact on women themselves.

HOOK-SWINGING

Before specifically addressing the practice of the Matikor/Dig Dutty ritual, we should mention two other Hindu rituals that have also fallen into disuse and that have some relevance insofar as they relate to the issue of fertility. We refer here to the ritual of hook-swinging, or the *charak puja*, and to Phagwah. Hook-swinging was a short-lived ritual in the Caribbean observed by people of lower castes. The ritual paid homage to the god Shiva and to Mother Durga, who were believed to offer protection to the ritual's participants during the process of "swinging" (Magru 2005). In exchange for being guaranteed children and a supply of rice, lower-caste Indians were obliged to become devotees of Shiva. Shiva, in turn, instructed the Bhagtas[3] on how to perform the *charak puja*.

> For three days prior to the ceremony, devotees must fast and observe certain ritual purity. During the ritual, the Bhagtas, adorned with garlands of flowers and with hooks impaled in the fleshy portions of their backs, were swung from the longer end of a stout pole pivoted on a firmly planted upright thirty to forty feet above the ground. In India, sometimes two beams instead of one were placed across the top of the pole to enable three or even four persons to "swing" at one time. The rotation usually lasted between two and five minutes accompanied by music, particularly the flute. (Magru 2005, 25–26)

Basdeo Magru notes that, given the perceived "cruel nature" of this ritual, it was the subject of considerable public condemnation, some of which suggested that the practice might have a bad effect on "young Creoles who witnessed the spectacle in significant numbers" (Magru 2005, 26). By the mid-1850s, the ritual of hook-swinging had been abandoned in Guyana.

PHAGWAH

The Phagwah festival, associated with the changing of the seasons around the world, is still celebrated in the Caribbean among people of Indian descent. In Guyana and Trinidad, the festival, known as Holi in some places, is celebrated on the day after the full moon in early March, around March 12. It is a festival of music, dancing, fertility, and harvest. Celebrants are covered with baby powder that has been dyed many different colors, and sometimes they are sprayed with colored water. Often, people throw baby powder on each other as part of the fun of the celebration.

The festival originates from a tale in Hindu mythology involving an evil king who despises his son, Prahlad, because Prahlad refuses to worship him. Prahlad venerates only Rama, Vishnu's incarnation on earth. The king tries to kill Prahlad with fire and is aided by his sister, Holika, who, believing herself to be immune to fire, sits in the flames with the child. When the flames subside, Prahlad emerges unharmed while his aunt perishes in the fire. The moral of the story is the triumph of good over evil.

The Phagwah festival is a manifestation of the continuation of an Indo-Caribbean identity in Guyana and Trinidad. It has endured from the period of indenture to the present. Not surprisingly, various aspects of the ritual have changed over time, and one could argue that the singing of traditional *chowtal* songs now shares musical space with contemporary chutney music. *Chowtal* is a recurring pattern or beat associated with Hindustani classical music. Moreover, a certain amount of creolization has taken place in the celebration of Phagwah in that the festival, perhaps more so in Trinidad than in Guyana, has attracted all classes and races of people and is no longer an exclusive celebration of Indo-Caribbean people. Furthermore, as Indo-Guyanese and Indo-Trinidadians migrate to Canada and the United States, the celebration of Phagwah has become an important cultural expression of identity and heritage in the diaspora. The diasporal reach of the Phagwah brings even more diversity to the celebration, which has been held (among other places) in Richmond Hill, New York City, for the past twenty-nine years. The celebration in Richmond Hill (a neighborhood in Queens) has attracted many different people, some of whom have family ties to the Caribbean and others for whom it is simply an occasion to celebrate the spring and have a good time.

An interesting development in the Richmond Hill Phagwah celebration is the participation of members of the Caribbean Equality Project—a Lesbian, Gay, Bisexual, and Transgender (LGBT) group. The inclusion of this group in the Phagwah is a testimony to the hybridization of the festival as it is practiced in the diaspora. We are not sure if such open participation of an LGBT group in the Phagwah would have been as easily embraced in Guyana or Trinidad, but we are cognizant of the fact that members of the LGBT community would have been a part of the celebration all along, if not openly. Lomarsh Roopnarine, writing in the *Guyana Times*, expressed the hope and frustration of the celebration of Phagwah in Guyana by concluding as a parting lament in his article: "There is no doubt that Holi breaks down walls of ethnic separation and brings us closer. I have witnessed all ethnic groups celebrating Holi in ways that would shock people from the Sub-continent, where ethnic and religion [*sic*] division is the norm rather than the exception. I wish my Guyana would feel like Holi every day, but this might be only a dream" (Roopnarine 2017).

MATIKOR

The Matikor/Dig Dutty ritual has not followed the same trajectory as hook-swinging or Phagwah in Guyana and Trinidad, perhaps largely because its practice did not raise eyebrows or attract the attention of the colonial authorities; it appeared much less "strange" than the other two practices. The term "Matikor" is made up of two words: *mati*, which means earth, and *kor*, which means digging. Matikor/Dig Dutty is a Hindu premarital ritual widely practiced in the Indian diaspora in the Caribbean, in places such as Guyana, Guadeloupe, Martinique, Trinidad, and Suriname. This chapter focuses on Dig Dutty/Matikor in Guyana and Trinidad. Sarita Boodhoo observed: "How this ceremony originated is not known but it is a long standing folk custom. It is not found in the scriptures themselves, but is mentioned in the Padhatis" (1993, 195). The Trinidadian Hindu scholar Ravi Ji also noted this point in his interview with us on June 19, 2002: "I have never found any mention of it in the Vedas; therefore I would say it started among the folk and then the ceremony graduated to be mentioned in the Padhatis and how to actually do it." Ji noted that, in time, scholars may have refined the ritual and integrated it more with tradition, in the process regularizing the practice in the Padhatis.[4] The Sanskrit term for this ritual is *mridaharana*, while in Bhojpuri it is known as *matkor*. We use both terms in this book, but generally Indo-Guyanese use the term Dig Dutty, while Indo-Trinidadians use the term Matikor. In both places, the activity constitutes a premarital ceremony known as Tilak. Although in India the ceremony varies from state to state, in Guyana and Trinidad it is remarkably consistent in practice. Pandit Persaud reported in an interview with us on June 12, 2003:

The intention is not simply to dig the earth. It is to adore, worship, and do homage to what we call *pitili mata*. We believe strongly that the earth is the greatest source of sustenance, and in a marriage life, the couple needs to be fed, to enjoy all of the things that are available in life, and we pay homage to Mother Earth in that context.

Matikor/Dig Dutty is an important procedural step in a Hindu wedding ceremony.

THE MECHANICS OF THE RITUAL

The Matikor/Dig Dutty ritual comes from the Vedic Hindu tradition that originated in northern India, interpreted from traditional Hindu writings, ancient texts, hymns, incantations, and rituals. The ritual is performed on the Friday before the wedding, which usually occurs on a Sunday. Traditionally, only women performed this ritual; men were considered marginal to the performance. The ritual is performed at the homes of both the *doolaha* (bridegroom) and the *doolahin* (bride). It is an expression of homage to Mother Earth, Vasu Mati/Mata, in which the couple must first seek the blessings of the earth for a successful and fruitful marriage. The ritual is seen as foundational to the Hindu philosophy of marriage. It begins with the mother of the bride or groom, along with four women, performing a *maandar puja* and then *teekaying* (marking with a dye) the drum. A drum always accompanies the singing of the songs in this ceremony. A mixture of *sindoor* (cosmetic powder), pan leaves with *sopari* (betel leaves), flowers, rice grains, and a coin is placed on the drum five consecutive times; the mixture falls to the ground and is collected in the *orhni* (head scarf) of the *doolaha*'s or *doolahin*'s mother. After the drummer is given a *seedha* (offering), he begins to beat the drum, as a way of calling the ancestors to witness the wedding. A tray is then prepared with such items as soaked dal or korma, a *deeya* with a wick and oil to be lit at the ceremony, *sindoor*, *hardi*, flowers, pan leaves, and some coins. The tray is covered with a yellow cloth, lifted up by five women, and placed on the head of a young girl, who transports the tray to the site of the ritual. This girl is usually a *phouphou* (an unmarried sister of the *doolaha* or *doolahin*), usually under ten years of age and presumed to be a virgin. If no *phouphou* is available, some other young girl carries the tray.

Sarita Boodhoo cites the Padhatis in describing the ritual: "In the Padhatis it is mentioned: On the ninth, seventh, fifth or third day before the marriage in an auspicious moment, with music and dancing, earth should be fetched from a place to the north or east of the house for growing sprouts, in a pot of clay or a basket" (1993, 195). The participants in this ritual walk from the house of the *doolahin* to the site of the of homage to the earth, involving the digging of the earth. In considering which direction the procession should take, the location of either the *doolahin* or *doolaha* is taken into account. Upon arrival at the location where the dirt is to be obtained, a hoe is ritualistically purified. Five *shognans* (women whose husbands are alive) mark the hoe to purify it, first washing the hoe and then applying *sindoor* (and *hardi*) to it. A participant uses the hoe to clear a patch of earth. The tray carried by the young girl is then placed on the ground, and the mother of the bride or groom sits on the ground and pours water on the patch of earth cleared by the hoe, smoothing it over with her hands. The contents of the tray are then emptied onto this ground, and the participants offer a puja to Mother Earth. In essence, the mother of the bride or groom is telling Mother Earth what is being done, asking her to leave the site where the digging has taken place and go to the home of the bride or groom to witness and honor the marriage ceremony. After the puja is finished, *sindoor* is applied to the foreheads of all the married women at the ceremony, and the korma (or whatever sweets have been brought to the ritual) is distributed to all in attendance at the ceremony. Pandit Persaud summarizes the ritual in the following manner:

> There are two aspects to Matikor in Guyana. One where the ladies go near to flowing water, probably a pond, somewhere like that; and there the mother of the bride or bridegroom do puja at that place to Mother Earth. In addition to the spiritual aspect . . . there is some degree of enjoyment, entertainment—they sing, they dance, they play the *tassa*, and they play music. They sing along the route. Then they return back to the home of the marriage, there the pandit takes over.

He performs a full puja. Two aspects have direct relation to this purpose. One is where the bride or groom, as the case may be, is given a *kangan. Kangan* is like a . . . suit of protective thread. It is made of a piece of yellow cloth. There is rice in it, grains, *chipari,* betel nut, flour . . . and then this is tied around the hand of the *doolahin* or *doolaha* as the case may be. (interview, June 12, 2003)

Persaud then went on to provide an explanation of the ritual belief system behind the protective symbolism and the importance of the *kangan* in the Hindu cosmology.

The belief is, it becomes a protective thread, to save the bride or groom, as the case may be, of any form of difficulty, problem, and usually to let them be protected to the end of the marriage, because that *kangan* which is tied with the recital of the appropriate mantra is only released or removed after the marriage ceremony. The practice and the tradition is, the bridegroom takes off the bride's [*kangan*] and the bride takes off the bridegroom's. That *kangan* is taken with other things that were used in the puja to the sea, and the mother leads an entourage, and they do what is called a Ganga puja. That is the practice in Guyana. (interview, June 12, 2003)

The second part of the Matikor/Dig Dutty ritual, described by Persaud in the above quotation, is done at the home where the marriage is to take place. The wedding party brings with them some of the earth that had been dug by the hoe, which is blessed by the pandit. The pandit then reads mantras; a goblet is placed on top of the earth, into which water is poured, and a bamboo and sucker plant are also placed on the same earth. According to Indrani Sharma:

After the ceremony at home, they bless the dye—ground turmeric mixed with oil—and that is applied [to the body]. Turmeric is an antiseptic by nature, it is a form of cleansing, and you [the bride or groom] sit there all by yourself, and they reminisce about their childhood and how they would be leaving that stage of life to enter into a different stage, which is called *grahistrasha.* (interview, June 10, 2003)

The ceremony at the site of the house is performed in praise of Lord Ganesha, the son of Shiva, a Hindu deity of knowledge and success, and a remover of all obstacles. All of the items used in the Matikor/Dig Dutty ritual have symbolic importance. The dye, for example, is for protection against evil and jealousy. As one woman in the Tain Settlement area of Berbice, Guyana, suggested: "You can't trust nobody" (focus group, June 12, 2003). There is some fear that wicked or jealous people can interfere with the future bride's happiness or even disrupt her ability to conceive a child. On one level, the songs that are sung at a Matikor/Dig Dutty ritual give instructions to the bride-to-be on how to protect herself from being ensnarled by those who might try to harm her or wish her ill. But there is also a sense of loss; according to Raymond Smith and Chandra Jayawardena: "Another group of women may chant songs of abuse about the bridegroom, who, they say, has come to steal away their daughter. These songs are gradually being forgotten and are rarely sung nowadays" (1958, 185). The bride and groom are left alone for a certain period, during which no one is to have any contact with them: "So yuh doh want anybody hit [touch] yuh" (Tain Settlement, focus group, June 12, 2003). Although the dye is applied to the body for protection, Pandit Persaud suggests that it is also anointing and invigorating for the bride and groom.

The grains that are used in the Matikor/Dig Dutty ritual also play an important role. While the grains signify the Indian community's foundation in agriculture, which goes all the way back to the beginning of the period of indenture in the Caribbean, Sarita Boodhoo (interview, June 14, 2003) has argued that, in addition they are offered as an oblation to the *vedi* (the small altar where the bride and bridegroom offer themselves in sacrifice to the fire god). The *vedi* is made of earth and is considered sacred. The rice grains, of various colors, are scattered over the earthen altar. In essence, there is an environmental and agricultural orientation to Matikor/Dig Dutty, and Pandit Persaud is again insightful in explaining this orientation: "You go to the Matikor, they plant a sucker. They plant a bamboo. And long time [long ago] they allow the sucker to grow and produce. Hence the concept of production and sustenance and feeding have had [*sic*] its reality intertwined in the ceremony itself" (interview, June 14, 2003).

Also worthy of note is that the actual Matikor/Dig Dutty ritual, the process of digging the earth with a hoe, is essentially a gendered practice. A married woman—usually the mother of the bride or bridegroom or a close relative—performs the digging. Therefore, Matikor is viewed predominantly as a female activity. The only men who play a designated role in Matikor/Dig Dutty are the *tassa* drummers. Initially, women even provided the music by beating the *dholak* drum, but *tassa* drummers, who are usually men, gradually replaced the women. The digging site is considered a female space, and men are only invited to participate in the marginal zones as drummers. However, Seligman and colleagues remind us of "the crucial role of music and rhythmical chanting or music in so many rituals, elements that have a deep emotional import not necessarily translatable into words but entraining the body and brain" (2008, 67). Nevertheless, given the designation of the Matikor/Dig Dutty ritual as a female space, men have not been encouraged to attend even as spectators, save for the *tassa* drummers, who are kept at some distance from the center of the digging. But while Matikor/Dig Dutty is still viewed as a female ritual, men are now being excluded less than before. As one respondent in Tain Settlement noted: "Long time weh dem ole people livin deh, man didn't go [to Dig Dutty] so much, but dis time hey now . . . [they attend]" (focus group, June 12, 2003). In the contemporary practice of Matikor/Dig Dutty, a theater of spectatorship has emerged, and men are present at the culmination of the ritual when there is dancing and drumming. Indeed, this celebratory part of the ritual, which was formerly hidden from public view, is now known to attract many onlookers—particularly men—who remain peripheral to the activity but who enjoy the dancing of the women. The dancing is often sexually suggestive, which perhaps explains its allure for some men. Men are not invited to dance in these suggestive ways; it is only the women who participate.

Gender is clearly an important part of this ritual, but ethnicity at times intercedes in unforeseeable ways. During a focus group session with about eight women in Tain Settlement in Guyana, one respondent who identified herself as Madrassi (a person whose ancestors came from the southern state of Madras) interjected: "Madras people don't have Matikor" (focus group, June 12, 2003). She suggested that, instead, Madrassis perform another kind of modified ritual: "Juss like Friday mornin, they does get the Pandit to give one lil speech and rub de dye, like . . . like Hindu people [do]. De same but in a different way. Like de ole generation dat come from India, so the new generation don't know bout dem Indian ting" (focus group, June 12, 2003). The woman was unable to articulate why Madrassi Indians in Guyana did not participate in Dig Dutty/Matikor. Writing specifically about Guyana, Stephanos Stephanides observes that laborers from the south of India were called "Madrassis": "The name refers to the fact that, in the nineteenth century, their ancestral villages in the Tamil region were contained within the Madras Presidency of British India, and to the fact that they embarked for the journey to South America from the port of Madras" (2000, 11). Although there are people of Madrassi descent in Trinidad, they are not known by that name, and the Kali temples were not yet established. Kali is an Indian folk goddess who is regarded as the mother force of the universe. To her followers, she is merciful and all suffering. Kali worship has its origin in West Bengal, where temples were dedicated to the worship of this goddess. In the 1970s, a group of *pujaris* (Hindu temple priests) from the Corentyne coast of Guyana, where Tain Settlement is located, went to Trinidad to "help establish Kali temples there; before this time, Kali worship in Trinidad was found only in families and small groups" (Stephanides 2000, 11–12).

The Matikor/Dig Dutty ritual originates in Vedic Hindu tradition, which is dominant in Guyana as it is in India. Many Guyanese Hindus, in fact, are so entrenched in the tradition that they believe that Vedic Hinduism is the only form of the religion practiced in Guyana. As Peter van der Veer and Steven Vertovec have observed: "In the Caribbean Hinduism differences in social and religious practice have been underplayed in the course of a long-term historical process in which a homogeneous Hindu community has been constructed" (1991, 149). Although people of Madrassi origin are Hindus, they do not practice Vedic Hinduism. The Vedic tradition is largely a northern construction. Madras, in the south of India, belongs to the Dravidian culture and languages, which many have argued predate the Vedic tradition.[5] Whereas the Vedic Hindu tradition honors the male deities of the Ramayana, Krishna and Vishnu, the Dravidian tradition pays homage to the goddess Kali. The Tain Settlement woman quoted above may simply have been discouraged, or she may have been pointing out her own nonparticipation in the Dig Dutty ritual without being able to explain the constraints that Hinduism as practiced in Guyana places on a Madrassi woman compared to her Vedic neighbors. Such divergence underscores the point made by van der Veer and Vertovec—that Hinduism in the Caribbean is heterogeneous.

There may be an even bigger distinction between the Vedic and Dravidian traditions within Hinduism with respect to the Dig Dutty ritual. Kali, the Universal Mother, is generally construed as the goddess of darkness. She is, in fact, very dark in complexion, as are most people who identify or are identified as Madrassi in Guyana. Kali is believed to be at the center of creation and destruction and is considered a source of cosmic energy. Madrassi Indians in the broader scheme of Guyana's Hindu religious tradition occupy a marginal space.

> Constituting a minority within an Indo-Caribbean Hindu majority in pre-independence Guyana, Madrasi Indians were relegated to the very fringes of cultural and religious marginality by Hindu high mindedness and colonial racism. Confined to limited paradigms of representation in terms of demography and cultural alterity, Madrasis were thereby subjected to the dual hegemony of racialized and ethnic difference that reinforced their minority status. (Mehta 2004, 542)

What is worthy of note here is that, although there are persons of Madrassi decent in Trinidad, the divergence between South and North Indians is not commonly viewed as an ethnic distinction. The descriptor "Madrassi," when used, is not so much an ethnic identifier as a geographic one, and the plurality if Hinduism in general is understated. In Guyana, on the other hand, the identifier "Madrassi" includes a social component that is recognized by the wider Indian community, and by broader Guyanese society.

Indeed, there may be other factors in play here in the reluctance of Madrassis to participate in Dig Dutty relating to matters of caste and color gradation. Brinda Mehta's observation is useful in this regard:

> Discriminatory practices based on skin coloring and the inherent Aryan belief in the primitiveness and cultural inferiority of non-Aryan social systems depicted Madrasis as cultural anomalies who were less Indian and therefore, less Hindu than the fair-skinned northerners from Uttar Pradesh and Bihar, thereby justifying their marginalization within the larger Indo-Caribbean community in British Guiana. (2004, 542)

Furthermore, proponents of Vedic Hinduism often make a point to distance the Dig Dutty ritual from Kali-Mai Puja, a Madrassi ritual that venerates Kali and seeks her blessings to promote fertility in women, healthy crops, and other benefits (Mehta 2004, 550). The Kali-Mai Puja ritual in contemporary practice has undergone some commingling with the obeah (necromancy or magic) rituals practiced by people of African descent—a fascinating topic in its own right. Keith McNeal observes that "those who castigate it [Kali-Mai Puja] as obeah often attribute Kali Worship to the legacy of darker-skinned Madrassis" (2011, 211).

It is therefore no surprise that Pandit Persaud, cited earlier in this chapter, objected to the term "ritual." In fact, he protested: "I don't like the word 'ritual.' Ritual connotes something that is superstitious and that sort of thing" (interview, June 14, 2003). Persaud's objection is understandable in anthropological terms. People who practice certain religious rituals always seek to distinguish themselves from other ritual practitioners, in order to avoid any misunderstanding.

The Matikor/Dig Dutty ritual essentially marks the transition from single life to married life. Ethnic Hindus, whether practicing their religion or not, participate in the ritual as an important initiation into married life. Only those ethnic Hindus who have become Christianized generally abstain from participating in Matikor/Dig Dutty. To forgo the ceremony—in the ethnic Hindu community—is to tempt fate with respect to the longevity and stability of one's marriage.

There are deeper layers of meaning in the ritual that go beyond its role marking a rite of passage. There is, for example, what Victor Turner (1969) calls "communitas"—a network of social relations wherein the liminal space provided by ritual forges a deeper bond that, at least temporarily, elides some existing differences such as class and status. However, not even the liminality of the sacredness of ritual seems a match for the issues of caste and gender. Indeed, Turner himself concludes: "[F]or individuals and groups, social life is a type of dialectical process that involves successive experience of high and low, communitas and structure, homogeneity and differentiation, equality and inequality" (1969, 97).

Within the context of the notion of communitas, Matikor/Dig Dutty also serves the pivotal function of reproducing cultural traditions among Hindus and thereby fortifying ethnic identity. In a racially plural society, diasporic Indians in Guyana and Trinidad hold on dearly to those cultural signifiers, myths, historical memories, traditions, and religious beliefs that continue to affirm their ethnic identities as Indian and Hindu. The production and reproduction of specific forms of Indian culture are vital to this communitas, which is always in danger of the ever-encroaching process of creolization. Mary Douglas's observations in this regard capture the extent and depth of the relationship established in the ritual: "The more personal and intimate the source of ritual symbolism, the more telling the message. The more the symbol is drawn from the common fund of human experience, the more wide and certain its reception" (2002, 141).

The Matikor/Dig Dutty ritual is therefore an important source of ethnic mobilization in both the Guyanese and Trinidadian contexts. Although the ritual has remained largely consistent in its practice over the years, there have been some modifications to some of the activities surrounding the ritual. For example, not many people go to a river to perform Matikor/Dig Dutty. Instead, they settle for a public standpipe. The ritual has become more public, including dancing in the village, in contrast to the more private observance of the ritual in the past. And the dimension of spectatorship, particularly to include male observers, is another modification of the ritual. In the end, however, Matikor/ Dig Dutty simultaneously offers continuity of religious practice and ethnic mobilization for Hindus in Guyana, Trinidad, and other places in the Caribbean where the ritual is performed.

The continuation of a ritual in a diaspora community always involves some degree of creolization, taking into account local conditions. Matikor/Dig Dutty has been more prone to creolization than most other rituals, since few Hindu immigrants could read the Padhatis. In order to learn the rituals, they had to depend on oral traditions. All the women we interviewed said that they learned the ritual from their elders: "My mudder use to carry me, we want to see so we went up front, I was with meh mudder and then I married nine churren" (Lakan Birju, interview, June 17, 2002). Another woman said that she learned to do the ritual "from me grandmudder, me mudder and me aunt, when they was in wedding procession dey use to take me along and I watch and learn" (Ruby Ragoonan, interview, June 16, 2002).

There is also much debate about whether the Matikor/Dig Dutty practice is a fertility ritual or not. Some have suggested that the digging of the dirt—and in times past the planting of sprouts—signifies fertility. There is some doubt about this position, because the planting of sprouts was a component of many other rituals as well. Others suggest that the sexually suggestive dance movements that the women perform can be interpreted as a fertility dance. Ruby Ragoonan, an elderly female respondent, put it this way: "Some of the ladies want to dance a little ridiculous, they want to shake up a little more; long ago those ladies had long *gangry* [skirts], they would roll up the *gangry* [in the shape of a penis] and they put it between deh foot [meaning their legs] and . . ." (demonstrating the action by gyrating her waist) (interview, June 16, 2002).

Indeed, many respondents pointed out that modernization is beginning to have an impact on the ritual; they mentioned that women now come in their "jeans and high heels." Moreover, some interviewees noted that the "wining" (sexually suggestive dancing) previously associated with carnival had not only infiltrated chutney but had now become part of the way the women dance.

Although today women dance like that in a wining country like ours, but within the ritual tradition it remains a pure festival—I am not sure if "pure" is the correct word. So even if you find that the people who are there have gone to carnival fetes or a chutney fete and they wine down on each other—today when they go there it is a ritual and if it [is] a little open they would not do it, but if it is a more closed place they would do it. (Ruby Ragoonan, interview, June 16, 2002)

In some cases, Matikor has become a site of racial interaction. The Matikor ceremony is one of the few places where Indo-Trinidadian Hindu women have interacted freely with African Trinidadian women. In Trinidad, up until the 1970s, there were few African Trinidadian participants in many of the Hindu rituals and festivals; generally, there was little interaction between the races. The older women we interviewed particularly noted that African Trinidadian women nowadays frequently participate in Matikor. One noted that, in time, more people would participate: "Any race can take part in it, long ago would have been only Indian people now it is more open, now yuh have Moslem people, Negro people, Christian people" (Lakan Birju, interview, June 17, 2002).

The Guyanese practice of Dig Dutty is in many ways much less creolized than the Matikor in Trinidad. Guyana has a much longer, stronger tradition of racial mobilization for political purposes, which has resulted in considerable acrimony between people of African and Indian descent. While there is some participation by African Trinidadians in Matikor, there is no such level of participation in Guyana. The ritual remains exclusively Indian, and largely private. The years of political strife between the principal races in Guyana essentially excludes people of African descent from any role in Dig Dutty. The process of creolization is much more advanced in Trinidad, where many of the major Indian rituals such as Diwali, Hosein, and Phagwah are so hybridized that they are no longer just Indo-Trinidadian festivals but broader Trinidadian occasions for celebration. Indeed, it is not uncommon to see African Trinidadians participating at the enactment of the story of Rama and Sita. We should, however, emphasize that the process of creolization in no way removes all tensions and conflicts between the two primary racial groups in Trinidad. Tensions indeed remain, but they seem to reach the boiling point less often than they do in Guyana. The Matikor ritual seems more fluid and perhaps a bit more inclusive in Trinidad, whereas in Guyana the long history of racial conflict and political mobilization around ethnic difference inhibits the participation of African Guyanese in the Dig Dutty.

The ceremony also provides a space for women of different ages and social backgrounds to interact with each other. In earlier times, when class differences were less prominent, Matikor was a space where many women would rekindle their friendships with others. With upward mobility, there are fewer spaces where middle-class Indo-Trinidadian women can interact freely with women of different classes, but at Matikor, if they choose to attend, they invariably rub shoulders with women of all classes.

In the case of Trinidad, certain changes came with modernization. Older women often feel that the younger generation flouts the rules. For example, they note that strict enforcement of the "no males rule" is no longer being followed at Matikor: "You can't control anything anymore, you see the men in front now, when you ask where yuh going they say what wrong with dat, now the parents saying let the boys come, the same ting he mooma have is the same ting we have so let him go and see" (Lakan Birju, interview, June 17, 2002). The same respondent complained:

> Now woman dressing more, they don't have the mind as to what dey doing, they know that the flowers is not to burn but dey going to throw [burn] it anyway, and they would say who tell yuh dat. Women don't like as I did anymore, well people don't believe on anything anymore, they are breaking all the traditions. The Matikor would continue but is how dey go do it. They would have the *kanya dan* [a sort of bracelet] and drink rum and beer; before you not suppose to even eat salt [in food] far less to drink rum. The old way was the best and the new way is no way. They only singing, dancing, and drinking rum and don't care, girl want to meet boy, they out all night talking, that is the fete now but long ago when ladies come to yuh house they sit down and sing and have competition. (Lakan Birju, interview, June 17, 2002)

Another respondent noted changes in the participation of the bride and groom: "Now the *doolahin* and *doolaha* does come and watch the dancing but long time you could not come out and see, you could not move around as you want in the past" (Ruby Ragoonan, interview, June 16, 2002).

As with the celebration of Phagwah by Indo-Caribbean people in the diaspora, particular cultural elements of the adoptive countries have come to influence the practice of Matikor/Dig Dutty, for example in Queens, New York, and Toronto. Sometimes, people attempting to re-create the ritual in the North American context are not always sure of the appropriate procedures. Often, elders having historical memory of the ritual are simply not there to ensure that the correct procedures are followed. Sometimes, a Hindu who has lived in North America for some time and adopted North American culture may call into question some aspects of the ritual. One resident of Hamilton, Ontario, declared: "I like to know that I'm doing things correctly. The things that don't make sense to me I may not do" (Lucknauth 2009). Beyond such concerns, however, is the tendency to treat Matikor/Dig Dutty as a form of entertainment, just another occasion to eat, drink, and dance. With the widespread availability of video recording devices, including cell phones, some Matikor/Dig Dutty celebrations are posted online as YouTube videos purely for entertainment purposes, stripping them of their ritualistic significance. Nevertheless, what is sociologically important here is the attempt, however acculturated, to ensure that an important ritual continues to be practiced at least in some form in the diaspora.

Finally, given the original moorings of the Matikor/Dig Dutty ritual in traditional agriculture, one might reasonably expect that its practice would fall off in the face of an increasingly modernized society. But this challenge of modernization to the relevance Matikor/Dig Dutty has not been significant. First, although many Indo-Guyanese and Indo-Trinidadians have become socially mobile, many others remain in a rural environment, still working in rice farming and sugar production. Second, even for those who are ensconced in the professions or civil service, Matikor/Dig Dutty continues to be an ethnically and religiously important tradition, especially in the racially polarized context of Guyana. We therefore have a slightly different sense of the arc of change than do Smith and Jayawardena, although some of our thinking about the significance and persistence of the ritual resonates with the following passage on other levels:

> The fact of performing this marriage ceremony at all is in itself symbolic of the participants' position in the Guianese [and, by extension, Trinidadian] social system. The strict performance of all the ritual actions involved in an orthodox wedding has its own value for the participants because it is thought to be the proper "Indian" way of doing things, irrespective of whether each element has meaning in itself. Not all Hindus marry according to Sanatan rites. Members of the reformist Arya Samaj specifically condemn some of the ritual elements such as the mati kore and the kichree ceremony, and exclude them from their wedding ceremonies. The exclusion of these allegedly "superstitious" or "uncivilized" elements becomes a symbol of "progressiveness" mainly in terms of Guianese [and Trinidadian] and Western European social values. Many of the more sophisticated middle-class Indians abandon the ceremony altogether in favour of a Christian marriage or combine it with such specifically Guianese [and Trinidadian] and European elements as a wedding reception with a cake, toasts, speeches, and ballroom dancing. (Smith and Jayawardena 1958, 191)

The Dig Dutty/Matikor ritual is an important part of Hindu ethnic identity. It is central to the story of historical displacement and reterritorialization, and it is a testimony to the tenacity of a people for whom such practices have long been seen, by many in the Guyanese and Trinidadian communities at large, as backward, pagan, and even a bit coarse. In the face of modernization, the Matikor/Dig Dutty ritual has shown remarkable resilience. But while modernity has not rendered Matikor/Dig Dutty irrelevant, the process of creolization has certainly modified some of the ritual's specific practices. Nonetheless, given its endurance as a symbolic practice, Matikor/Dig Dutty demands much more scholarly attention than it has received to date.

4

Indo-Guyanese Men

*Negotiating Race and Masculinity
in Contemporary Guyana*

The lived, everyday experience of masculinity in Guyana has yet to be fully articulated. Who men are, and what is expected of them, is a difficult concept to grasp and interpret. Gendered identities are never straightforward; rather, they are complex and multilayered. Determining a comfortable space in which to express one's gendered identity is hard enough, but doing so in the context of competing racial identities is that much harder. Nothing about defining social identity in Guyana has ever been easy. It is a country with a long history of racial turmoil. When gender is combined with race, negotiating the terrain of identity becomes a highly charged and contested process. Defining masculinity in racial terms is inevitably associated with a social context in which race structures political participation, affects one's perception of the distribution of economic resources, and decidedly influences access to power, privilege, and status.

The colonial project in Guyana prefigured the racialization of the country in much the same way that it did in other parts of the Caribbean. However, given the multiracial character and dynamics of Guyana and the divide-and-conquer policies of the colonial power, the racial legacy bequeathed to the society made political mobilization along racial lines an inevitable outcome. The impact of indenture had a lasting effect on those countries where Indian labor was imported to shore up the labor supply. In the postemancipation period in the Caribbean, the establishment of free villages by the formerly enslaved, and the withdrawal of labor from the estates, necessitated the acquisition of labor from outside the region. The bulk of such labor was imported from the hill country of southern India. This movement of people was part of a significant migratory trend from India not only to the Caribbean but also to Mauritius, Fiji, southern and eastern Africa, and Sri Lanka. British Guiana imported 238,909 Indians; another 143,939 were sent to Trinidad. The first group of Indians arrived in Guiana in May 1838, on a five-year contract. During the period of their indenture, they could not leave their employer or refuse to do the work that was assigned to them. Walter Rodney's description of the working conditions of the indentured laborers is worth noting here in that they resembled the labor conditions of the African enslaved who preceded them:

> Periods of absence from work (when proved in court) and terms of imprisonment were excluded when calculating the five-years of the indenture bond. Apart from serious illness, the indentured immigrant placed his labor power at the unqualified disposal of the employer for every working day of the five-year period. This the law guaranteed. The law also helped to create a situation in which planters could increase the intensity of exploitation of indentured labor by using their power to define a "task." (1981, 42)

Rodney's observation about the heterogeneous nature of this group is also significant not only with respect to the indentured population but also more generally to the broad swath of Indo-Guyanese men discussed in this chapter: "As would be expected, each racial group had its own internal divisions. Indians did not constitute a homogenous group. They too faced problems deriving from religious, linguistic, cultural, and social difference brought from India" (1981, 185).

Clem Seecharan draws our attention to an important dimension in the shaping of identity during indenture:

> Narratives of India have been the most instrumental factor in the shaping of Indian identity in British Guiana (Guyana since May 26, 1966). From the beginning of indentureship to the present, diverse conceptions of homeland—"many Indias"—have been central to redefinition of self. It seems that however strong the sense of belonging to the new land has become, the necessity to look back, to create Indias of the mind, is inescapable. Becoming Indo-Guyanese, therefore, required the embracing simultaneously of multiple, often imaginary and contradictory, constructions of that homeland. Fact, fiction and fantasy are necessarily interlaced in reclaiming and reshaping identity. (2001, 1)

Seecharan goes on to argue that a mythical past "that speaks of ancient glory, preferably, a golden age" (2001, 2) becomes a necessity. He also notes that a certain amount of selective amnesia tinges the exercise of nostalgic glory.

As Francisco Scarano noted about the impact of indentured laborers, "their presence caused meaningful and lasting changes in the ethnic and linguistic character of these societies" (1989, 60). Difference and diversity inevitably brought conflict between the formerly enslaved and the more recent indentured Indians. Fomented by colonial policy and practice, these conflicts became deep divisions, with their fullest expression in the split of the nationalist movement in the early 1950s and with a continued legacy today between African and Indo-Guyanese.

Ever since the split in the nationalist People's Progressive Party (PPP) in 1953, race has been the lens through which everything in Guyana is filtered. It is in this context that we must examine how Indo-Guyanese men think about who they are, how they behave, and the role they see themselves performing in society. This chapter is based on observations made by men about masculinity in the Indian community in Guyana, gathered in a series of in-depth interviews and focus groups with men in Guyana in 2003 and again in 2013.

The Indo-Guyanese men we talked to clearly gave some thought to how they defined their masculinity, invariably taking their racial identity into account in doing so. One respondent believed that his Indian masculinity was special and important to him. He reflected: "I consider it a matter of pride, considering the society that we live in and that our foreparents are from India" (Versailles, focus group, July 2013). Following up on this comment, another young man was even more specific about the pride he felt in his ancestry: "It all comes down to our culture and from our foreparents, because they came as indentured servants, and as we are the offspring of them, I am proud to say that we have done a lot so far" (Versailles, focus group, July 2013). In terms of how they view themselves as Indo-Guyanese men, one respondent noted: "We don't have to prove or go out proving our masculinity to anybody. We are very restrainful [sic]. We don't have to go out and get into a fight. We are logical thinkers. This type of thinking that we have, 'don't get in trouble' kind of thinking that we have, defines a man more." Another added, "You kind of think through things more" (Versailles, focus group, July 2013).

Providing more detail about the character of Indo-Guyanese men, one man attempted to offer a more sophisticated explanation:

> I think Indian men are very cultured, despite again, shortcoming. There is an issue of alcohol consumption among Indian men, which is seen as a major problem. But despite all of that, you would find an Indian man, whatever religion he is. . . . For example, this is the month of Ramadan, even if this man drinks twelve months a year, in the month of Ramadan, you'll find him restraining for that month. For a Hindu man, he might be a cane cutter who drinks a lot, but if there is a Jhandi or Matikor or wedding or something like that, he has to restrain. There is a strong cultural connection . . . as against some other races, "oh, whatever happens, you know, there is no need for fasting, there is no need for restraint" . . . you'll find that the seriousness is not there. (Versailles, focus group, July 2013)

There is an automatic, underlying reproach of non-Indian men in the above passage, irrespective of their actual traits. Non-Indian men, in this narrative, are inherently morally degenerate. It is not surprising that some Indo-Guyanese men harbor notions of their own whole-someness in contrast to the flawed character of others. Guyanese colonial policy as well as its literature are replete with such spurious comparisons. Juanita De Barros notes how the Reverend J. G. Pearson described Africans as lazy and as "barbarians without history" while viewing the "East Indian" and "his wife as good parents who raised their son to prosperous and reproductive manhood" (De Barros 2014, 51). The specter of race continues to undergird much of the understanding of Indo-Guyanese masculinity. Note the following observation, for example: "You might see men of other races who see Indian men as weak, physically. They think you can't fight or some-thing like that" (Versailles, focus group, July 2013). Despite the attempt to distinguish Indians from "other races," at a very basic level this characterization of masculinity is rooted more traditionally in men's corporeality. It resides in brawn and strength and, in the end, does the opposite of what it seems intent on doing, namely, distinguishing Indo-Guyanese masculinity from other forms of masculinity.

Perhaps the corporeal is more readily discerned in the follow-ing observation from a young Indo-Guyanese man whose racial and sexual angst was quite palpable:

> Sometimes, I hear [that] other races look down on Indian men, and sometimes this even comes from women [of other races]. They say that Indian men are not overly endowed, and that is the particular reason a woman might choose another race. In Guyana, there is a saying: "She leaves the Indian man for better length as against better-ment." It gets even more intense if it was an Indian girl and an Indian man and if she left, for example, for a Negro fellow, then I become the laughingstock of everybody.
>
> You become the laughingstock within your own race. It is even more embarrassing because Indian people now start making fun of you. They laugh at you because you couldn't satisfy your woman and because she ran off with a black man. (Versailles, focus group, July 2013)

The above observation is remarkably revelatory. It is preoccupied with comparing the physical and sexual endowments of Indo-Guyanese and African Guyanese men, no doubt embracing the stereotype of the latter as possessing penises, as Stuart Hall once remarked, "as big as cathedrals" (1996). In addition, in an attempt to compensate for perceived sexual inadequacy, the respondent cites an ethnic aphorism suggesting that there is a zero-sum trade-off between sexual endowment and satisfaction vis-à-vis security and stability. Note here also the gendered valuation of abandonment. The blow is most crushing when an Indian woman, the embodiment of Indian culture and the agent of the socialization of children, leaves her partner for an African Guyanese man. The spurned man becomes an object of ridicule not only outside his racial group but within it as well. This fear of abandonment symbolizes both social embarrassment and perhaps recognition of the other, whom the Indo-Guyanese man may not necessarily always consider his equal. The anguish is not the same if an Indo-Guyanese man leaves a marriage for an African woman. "If an Indian man walks around with a Negro girl, he is seen as macho. Sometimes you could be walking on the road and the fellows would say, 'Wah you doing wid de coolie man?'" (Versailles, focus group, July 2013). Not to be missed in this comment is the use of the term "Negro"—an archaic word in most North American and European contexts but that continues to have currency in the Anglophone Caribbean, not just in Guyana but in Trinidad as well.

On another level, Indo-Guyanese men define their gendered identity in much the same way as other Caribbean men, and like men of other races they often have difficulty putting their lived experiences into words. This was particularly noticeable among the poor, working-class men we talked to around Berbice. Take the example of an Indo-Guyanese man in Tain Settlement: "De only ting me go say mek is a man is to have work, to mek yuhself as a man" (focus group, June 12, 2003). Masculinity and manhood are seen here as being fulfilled almost exclusively through work. Of course, despite what this respondent thinks of the ideal, he is acutely aware that work is not always available and therefore draws attention to the consequences of not living up to this role.

> So, like how aah we sit down here now. I come to aah we. We sit down,
> we gaff and taalk. Awright, yes. Say look, meh nah get job. Meh nah

get nuttin. But yuh got to look fuh job but job ain't deh in hay. Yuh caan get job.

[Another respondent chimes in] So yuh become a waste man. As a job yuh nah get job so yuh sit down waste. People check yuh like a waste. (focus group, June 12, 2003)

The above expression of this expected role is in itself rather interesting. Work is clearly foundational to these respondents' identity as men, but the reality is that most work around Tain Settlement is seasonal, based on the sugar industry. Men, therefore, experience long out-of-season periods of unemployment. This failure to provide for their families weighs heavily on their sense of self-worth; their inability to find work in the off-season is considered a "waste," and, by extension, an embarrassment and a mark of worthlessness. Despite their diminished masculinity engendered by unemployment, these men, like others in similar predicaments, realize that their inability to perform a particular role does not change the fact that they are men, and so they have to find strategies to adjust. Barry Chevannes's observations about the Indian family structure establish the general context in which Indo-Guyanese masculinity is defined and to which it is beholden:

The family structure itself is strongly patriarchal, with the ideal being a joint extended family. As the head and supreme authority, the male's main responsibility is to provide for his wife and children. His duty is to bring in the money, while that of his wife is to wash, cook, take care of the children, and to see the general upkeep of the house, including responsibility for the purchase of food and other necessities. As his children get old enough, his sons bring in their wives to live, while his married daughters go off to live in their fathers-in-laws' homes. His authority extends over his sons and their families as well. When he dies, his eldest son becomes head of the family. (2001, 70)

Chevannes's description might be modified to fit more contemporary situations, which often include Indo-Guyanese women participating in the workforce, not only contributing to the rearing and social reproduction of the family but also making significant contributions to the economic needs of the household. But while one might argue that some of the patriarchal characteristics outlined by Chevannes have changed, the Indo-Guyanese family remains largely patriarchal in its structure. One respondent makes the point quite clearly: "We view women as up there. Not necessarily equal but we give them the reverence" (Versailles, focus group, July 2013). There is a grudging acknowledgment that women are not seen as equal to men, despite a certain degree of reverence. A young Indo-Guyanese, middle-class man offered the following observations about his understanding and experience of family:

> Well, when it comes to family, that institution in particular, from my experience, I think an Indian man has a sense of responsibility toward his family, children, and acquisition of wealth. If we were to make comparisons to other men, you might find other races in a sense, or other men, who are capable of doing the same thing, but they don't. And for whatever reason . . . Indian men, despite some shortcomings, they focus on building a family, they focus on responsibility to children and education, and things like getting a house, and acquisition of wealth. (Versailles, focus group, July 2013)

By unpacking some of the sentiments expressed in the above comment, we discover a number of traits that distinguish male Indo-Guyanese identity. First is the clear concern for family and property, a concern that is presented as though it were exclusive to Indian men. Second is the need to tease Indian men out of the larger male crowd. In our experience interviewing Indo-Caribbean men, statements about "other men" and "other races" are very often indirect references to African Caribbean or African Guyanese men. Indians in fact seem unable to avoid making such comparative references, however indirectly. Once "other races" have been thus identified, one must point out their differences, or shortcomings, in relation to Indian men. Some behavior or characteristic must set Indian men apart from men of "other races," who may have the wherewithal to be responsible fathers and providers but who somehow lack the discipline or moral fiber needed to undertake such tasks.

The Berbice area has a long-standing, middle-class Indian presence. Raymond Smith provides a sense of the nature of this Indian community:

> They [the Indian middle class] were instrumental in forming some of the earliest Indian organizations such as the British Guiana East Indian Association, which was formed in 1916 in Berbice and later extended to become a colony-wide organization centred on Georgetown. The objects of Association were "upliftment" of the Indian race and the securing of political representation in order to redress some of the grievances felt by Indian workers. (1964, 109)

The Berbice area has provided ample racialized social and cultural experiences to its Indian population to work into particular understandings of masculinity. Nevertheless, with the decline of the sugar industry, Tain Settlement, a rural community in Port Mourant, Berbice, has largely become a poor, working-class area, characterized by high unemployment—especially among men—and offering few avenues for mobility.

Rishee Thakur, a University of Guyana lecturer and Berbice resident, provides a clear picture of the role of race in Tain Settlement. Thakur's social class and education give him a different perspective from the men quoted earlier who work in the sugar industry:

> Certainly, there is no question about that [the fact that race enters his understanding of masculinity]. It's a bit mythological but real at the same time. I don't know if you know the story of the Mahabharata. The story of the Mahabharata, the character there is Arjuna. And I not only appreciate the debate between him and Krishna before the battle.... Arjuna goes to the end of the line and he says sorry my friend, I can't fight this battle here because if I do, over there I am going to have to kill my teachers and my cousins.... How is death to be justified in that context? Krishna turns to him and says, "Ah, see my friend, you do have a problem. Justice now name uncle; truth and honesty mean cousin." I have always latched onto the story because Arjuna is now going to be convinced of what he hears. Here was someone that I

had latched onto since I was a youth as a kind of a model of a person who had an awareness of his public duty, which came uppermost in his mind. And I have always found an easy alignment with that. But I don't know if that transforms it into something necessarily ethnic. (interview, June 12, 2003)

The Arjuna story touches on a major theme in how one defines oneself as a man, in this case an Indian man. There are other interpretations of the story than the one offered by Thakur. He was mindful of the problematic readings of this mythological story, but at its core, he saw Arjuna's crisis as one of identity: Arjuna must make a decision about who he is and what he must do based on that definition. Arjuna's dilemma, then, as Thakur points out, is an ethical one of devotion to family versus a commitment to duty or dharma, and to the necessity to act or karma. Ethically, we believe that Thakur is pointing to the complexity of identity that Amartya Sen alluded to, discussed above, which poses a dilemma for some men. In short, despite the emphasis on family in Indo-Guyanese communities, Thakur is offering a more nuanced explanation of masculinity that goes beyond simply a preoccupation with family, although that remains an important part of Indian men's lives, to embrace a broader set of issues—commitment to community, society, country, the environment—that could also be part of how Indo-Guyanese men construct their masculinity. This more expansive interpretation of masculinity is also in the end a call to action, as Arjuna eventually realized, requiring that Indo-Guyanese men, and indeed all men, must act in the interest of the greater good, not just for themselves.

Some Indian men in Tain Settlement, however, see no significant difference between themselves and men of other races. One respondent remarked: "Indian, black, Chinee [Chinese], coolie, Potagee [Portuguese], everybody is human being . . . is a person, right?" (focus group, June 12, 2003). It should be noted, however, that given their rural location, and given that their community is almost exclusively made up of people of Indian descent, these men have little point of reference of other races. In mixed communities and urban settings, racial lines are often more clearly defined; there is a greater sense of Indian masculinity being defined not merely in relation to African masculinity but in opposition to it. It is therefore instructive to consider the following comment of a woman in Tain Settlement addressing the issue of difference among Indian men: "Yes, in good action in good ways, yuh know. Well, not aall, aall o' dem. So, some ignorant" (focus group, June 12, 2003). We will return to this point below. When asked what sorts of developmental markers identified masculinity, one Tain Settlement respondent offered a very traditional understanding of the concept:

> In our culture here, one of the things that identifies a male person as being a man, is the first thing he is to demonstrate is that you have responsibility as a young man in the family. And the next step is that you feel you are mature enough yuh get married. When you get married, to prove your manhood, you want to be a father. And people look upon you as being a man. (focus group, June 12, 2003)

This response begs the question: What if you don't produce a child? Is your status as a man damaged or diminished as a result? The same respondent noted: "Very often in these parts of Guyana [Berbice], you find fatherless males." The respondent is referring to men who have no children, implying that there is some deficit of masculinity associated with the failure to father a child. In response to a question about the impact of this failure to live up to community expectations, our respondent opined: "They don't as an individual feel less of themselves [because they are not fathers], but because of peer pressure and gossips in the neighborhood and things like that, they would tend to feel themselves less of a man" (focus group, June 12, 2003).

Although for many there are definite responsibilities that come with the status of being a man, Thakur raised a seldom-articulated point about the interconnection of masculinity and femininity that adds some nuance to the issue. He reflected:

> I don't know if it has any . . . let's call them foundational statuses or ontological ones. I don't know if there are any. I grew up in a household where the most important persons in my life were not men but

four women ... my grandmother, my mother, my aunt, and my sister. Unfortunately, one of them is now dead, my grandmother, but my mother, my aunt, and my sister are still there and they still perform that function. If we were to take that as an indication, then no, I don't attach any particular function to being male. That's an open-ended question and that would be resolved in the context of your relations with other males and females. (interview, June 12, 2003)

Thakur is tapping into an important feature of the construction of masculinity in general here, namely that masculinity is defined in relation to femininity as well as in opposition to it. Gender identity is a dialectical relationship among men, women, and transgendered individuals. As for the specific issue raised by Thakur above, Linden Lewis observed: "Masculinity also has much to do with men's relationships to women. There is a sense in which men in society collectively define masculinity for themselves, but they are always cognizant of the influence of women in their definition. In short, women help to shape the general terrain of masculinity" (2003, 95).

In contrast, however, one female respondent from Tain Settlement had a very specific sense of the role of men in society. She argued: "When deh married deh got fuh work, we be de housewife. They go ah work a money and bring ah we and we got to control ah we self ... control ah de house an de money. Well me, me ah control me husband money" (focus group, June 12, 2003). This comment resonated with some of the respondent's male community members who had earlier placed emphasis on the ability of men to work. Here, however, work is not merely a desirable objective but rather a duty, and for the respondent this should not lead automatically to a sense of entitlement but should be viewed instrumentally such that the woman retains the right to control the household finances. One Indian man argued: "Meh ain't tink dat man should do house work all de time. Like when me wife sick or so" (focus group, June 12, 2003). This was an interesting concession. In effect, doing work in the homes where men live is not their primary responsibility, but under certain conditions, illness for example, they are prepared to chip in. This assistance only lasts as long as it takes for the wife or other responsible woman in the household to recover from her illness. Not surprisingly, there seems to be a social pact whereby at least some women agree to this form of contingent assistance. One woman echoed the point made by the man above: "Yes, like when meh sick or so, he does help meh. Meh does suffer with high pressure, yuh know. Like if meh come home and meh sick he does help meh cook. He does carry meh doctor and ting. He does tek care o' me" (focus group, June 12, 2003). The assumption of responsibility associated with Indian masculinity seems to differ little from that of other races of men in the Caribbean insofar as it is determined by patriarchal norms and is negotiated and fashioned in certain situations with considerations of pathos. The female respondent above acknowledges that housework is the woman's responsibility. She is fine with her husband assisting her, but not as a member of the family who is expected to contribute to the maintenance of the household on an ongoing basis.

Indian men in Guyana, like other men in the region, have long lived with stereotypes about who they are and how they behave. Indo-Guyanese men are almost always conceived of as rural dwellers who orient toward agriculture, specifically rice farming. In short, they are considered "country folk," and with this broad generalization they are seen as premodern and insufficiently educated. Much has changed in the postindependence period to call into question this kind of thinking. Many also view Indian men as overly thrifty, sacrificing even their own health in the pursuit of land, other property, or economic enterprise. Some find this notion of Indo-Caribbean asceticism problematic and unsociable. Brackette Williams notes this point in her distinction between making a living and making a life:

Most often, when they [Guyanese people] refer to someone's ability to make a living, they are speaking of the person's industry, skill and ambition, all of which result in material rewards. When they speak of someone's ability to make a life, they are referring to their own assessment of the individual's interest in the socioeconomic well-being of others and his inclination to balance work against sociability—the enjoyment of life through participation in organized and casual forms of socializing, on the one hand, and conspicuous consumption on the other hand. (1991, 56)

Even as Indo-Guyanese men define their own masculinity, they are often viewed in different ways by society. Among the stereotypes associated with Indian men is their alleged love of alcohol. Indian men indeed have a reputation for consuming significant amounts of alcohol, but more important in the macho Caribbean culture is the accusation that they are unable to manage their consumption. Such perceptions are often combined with another stereotype of Indian men being prone to violence, especially that which is alcohol induced and directed at women. There is no denying that heavy drinking is a problem among Indian men generally in Guyana. One female respondent was quite clear about her abhorrence of excessive drinking:

> Yes, lota problems. When he sobah [sober] he like to wuk hard. Meh could leff he and gone anyway, any day, any work, anyway meh want to go, he neva stop me, but when he drink rum, he does destroy. Every thing meh ah get if he see am, he want am. . . . But when he sobah he very good.
>
> If meh brother give me some money, ah have to gih he some part fuh he to drink, if not he make a problems wid me. . . . As soon as he drink a rum so, problems! Nobody doesn' like fuh dey husband drink rum. (focus group, June 12, 2003)

It was not clear if the respondent, using the word "destroy," was referring only to property or if she was implying domestic abuse—we did not pursue this point, to avoid any embarrassment it may have caused in the presence of other women. Admitting that there was indeed a problem with alcohol abuse among Indian men, Rishee Thakur had a particular reading of the problem: "[Alcohol abuse] is only symptomatic. It is not the real cause. It is the absence of adequate recreational cultural facilities in the community. There is nothing. . . . [T]he only thing that you will find between this community here and Skeldon, which is about twenty-five miles away, is the rum shop" (interview, June 12, 2003). To add to Thakur's point, we should also note that it would be unfair to see the problem of alcoholism as exclusive to Indo-Guyanese and Indo-Trinidadian men. Alcoholism is both a national and a regional problem in the Caribbean. Perhaps a lasting testimony to this fact, and a comment on Caribbean masculinity besides, is the Mighty Sparrow's calypso "Rum Is Macho," in which he makes a case for rum over other, competing liquors. One is perhaps able to sense the feeling of anguish that habitual rum drinking elicits from those who recognize the problem, but it should certainly not be labeled as a purely Indian male character flaw. One respondent noted: "They see Indian men as the rum suckers. They would blame rum for why his wife left him or his house fell apart" (focus group, June 12, 2013).

Barry Chevannes's findings regarding the practice of rum drinking in Guyana are particularly germane here:

[M]anhood is determined by a number of other social behaviours typical of adult males. Among these is the participation in and maintenance of male bonding activities, particularly public drinking. When a young man is able to do this without sanction, he is a man, regardless of his marital status.

"He gat rum! He loves rum!" With these words Gopaul [an informant] declares the diagnosis of his son's problem. Heavy drinking of alcohol is a male pastime in Overflow, particularly in its concentrated rum form. [Chandra] Jayawardena . . . calls it an example of the hedonism he found among unskilled estate labourers in Guyana. In Overflow beer is also consumed, but rum is the preferred drink. It is central to the festivities that accompany the life cycle rituals, and to male bonding among adults, young and old. [Informant] Praka's problem, however, and that of some others, was not only that he drank heavily, with all the expenses that that implies, but also that he would lose control and get into brawls. We may thus distinguish, as the Overflow community does, "drinking" from "having a drinking problem." Drinking is an institutionalized form of recreation for men, but it is also an important adjunct to all festivities, including all but one of the life cycle rituals. A drinking problem manifests itself when it goes beyond the established boundaries of drinking, both as to frequency and occasion, as well as to proper conduct. (2001, 87)

In constructing their masculinity, men of Indian descent in Guyana are often forced to confront these stereotypes, which become embedded as racial markers in the context of a multiracial society, ultimately assuming political implications which in turn separate communities. Negative characterizations of Indian men, whether real or imagined, can then be manipulated for social or political reasons, and certain cultural practices become a zone of contestation.

Thakur, in his comments on the subject of Indo-Guyanese masculinity, raised a perceptive point about the nature and practice of patriarchy within this community:

> [The traditional role of the Indian male] ... is very patriarchal in that sense and the East Indian middle class was very good at reproducing it. The irony is that precisely what was the strength of the Indian community, that is, the capacity to be able to hold things together, is also its soft underbelly because that is also where much of the abuse stems from, and stems from what many people view as this need for internal unity—to keep the family together at all costs. As soon as you start to ask that kind of question you get marginalized because you no longer serve what is going on here. And this is the irony, and the difficulty is that not very many folks want to speak to that, ... that there is such a high degree of suicide in East Indian communities ... and interestingly again, it's among East Indian men ... because they are somehow not allowed to express this sense of weakness they face in the presence of this all-powerful, all-knowing patriarchy. (interview, June 12, 2003)

Once again, Thakur is raising the complexity about masculinity that he referred to in relation to Arjuna's ethical dilemma. Thakur's perception of the inherent contradiction of patriarchal rule is important, and the problem has perhaps not received as much attention as it should. What Thakur calls the "soft underbelly" of the Indian community can more appropriately be described as a site of vulnerability of patriarchy, in which "the need to hold things together," as he observes, elicits increasing resistance to such control. The inherent contradiction, therefore, is that patriarchy seeks to eliminate opposition to its rule, but its authoritarian practices generate unending resistance at every level from the very constituencies it seeks to harness, namely women and marginalized men. What Thakur might be pointing to is the fact that the historical circumstances in which patriarchy has operated have changed, but the practice of domination continues to operate in the interest of reproducing power and privilege while attempting to ignore the dialectics of the forces of change. In this context, patriarchy seeks to increase its oppressiveness, but the opening space of autonomy provided by new circumstances simultaneously resists these efforts to turn back the hands of time. It is perhaps this inability on the part of Indo-Guyanese patriarchy to manage the discontent, regardless of what mechanisms of oppression it employs, that leads to the sort of alienation that Thakur believes results in suicide among Indian men.

Finally, in a polity characterized by the long and central presence of African Guyanese—a political culture dominated by black leaders in government, in the military, in society—black masculinity looms large in the construction of Indo-Guyanese masculinity. Defining Indo-Guyanese masculinity necessarily occurs in a racially charged environment in which race plays an inevitable role in how men view themselves and what claims and expectations society places on them. Any consideration of Indo-Guyanese masculinity operates on a mindscape of the perceived hegemony of African Guyanese and, more generally, African Caribbean masculinity. African Guyanese and African Caribbean masculinity simultaneously set the parameters for Indo-Guyanese masculinity as well as its point of departure. Whether explicitly or implicitly, Indian men in Guyana almost always refer to some characteristic of African Guyanese male behavior in describing who they are or what they consider important to do as men. As noted earlier, often they speak of "other men," which is usually a coded expression for "black men." In addition, although clearly family is of primary importance to Indian men, they speak of their commitment to the values of family life in ways that supposedly distinguish them from their African Guyanese counterparts.

What is also striking about Indian men's references, whether implicit or explicit, to men of African descent is the alarming certitude and the lack of nuance in their allegations of moral deficiency in their African counterparts. Surely, all African Guyanese men cannot be categorized with such uniformity, all with the same foibles. Indian men's failure to acknowledge any heterogeneity among men of African descent is as problematic as non-Indians' stereotyping of Indian men as prone to alcoholism and violent abuse of their wives and families. To engage in such vitriol is to revert to a much earlier colonial discourse about the inadequacy and inferiority of the people of the New World.

It would be difficult to ignore the racial differences that colonial powers emphasized in their imposition of slavery and indenture—differences they exacerbated and exploited in the interest of reproducing surplus value for the plantocracy. It would be equally remiss not to acknowledge the ways in which race-based political mobilization in Guyana further created rifts between people of African and Indian descent. It is within this milieu that long-held mythologies of black male sexuality create tensions between competing racialized forms of masculinity. This competition results in Indian men's preoccupation with policing the boundaries of female Indian sexuality and autonomy, in the interest of protecting the integrity of the family. We do not intend to suggest that Indo-Guyanese masculinity is a mere reaction to African Guyanese masculinity but rather to propose that unraveling the discourse on racialized masculinity in Guyana dictates that we be mindful of how different expressions of masculinity shape and influence each other. Moreover, evolving circumstances call for new responses and therefore different expressions of Indian masculinity, and of masculinity in general. In this way, we might begin to make sense of the extreme emphasis Indo-Guyanese men place on such matters as family, religion, work, and industry, as a means of distinguishing themselves from their biggest rivals, African Guyanese men, and perhaps African Guyanese people in general. Recognizing and acknowledging the historical moment can also go a long way toward helping us understand why Indian men construct their masculinity in the ways that they do.

5

The "New Indian Man"

Notions of Masculinity among Indo-Trinidadian Men

In 2004, the calypsonian Saucy (Denise Belfon) sang that she was "looking for ah Indian man," one that was "rough and sexy smart and cute." Forty-five years earlier, in 1959, another calypsonian, Skipper (Hubert Smith), described a completely different Indian man named Ramjohn. Ramjohn could not speak English properly; he used "green verbs" and demonstrated total ineptitude in the use of the language. Ramjohn went to Laventille, a neighborhood on the outskirts of Port of Spain predominantly inhabited by African Trinidadians, to learn to speak grammatically correct English. Clearly, Ramjohn was uneducated, devoid of any useful abilities (according to the intellectual expectations of creole Trinidad), and most certainly not a person to be emulated by African creole culture. In fact, he was to be ridiculed. Saucy is not looking for a Ramjohn; rather, she seeks a different kind of Indian man, one who has begun to assume new characteristics that Trinidadian society has not previously associated with Indo-Trinidadian men. What is this new type of Indian man who is beginning to emerge in society? This chapter explores changing notions of masculinity among Indo-Trinidadian males as the processes of globalization and modernization intensify in Trinidad. Indo-Trinidadian men are redefining their own perceptions of masculinity and how it is portrayed and exhibited. Their redefinition, however, is contradictory. At times, it is in opposition to African Trinidadian masculinity, while at other times it appropriates some dimensions of that same masculinity. Sometimes it challenges the traditional Indo-Trinidadian patriarchy, and sometimes it reinforces certain dimensions of the same traditional patriarchy. The creolization process is influenced not only by race and gender but also by class. Young, upwardly mobile Indo-Trinidadian men are refining their notions of masculinity by borrowing from external sources, drawing particularly on the influences of Hollywood and Bollywood. Traditionally, the creolization of Indo-Trinidadian men has been characterized as a top-down, one-way process; Indo-Trinidadian masculinity was described as a reaction to its African Trinidadian counterpart. Recently, however, the reverse has also been true: Indo-Trinidadian masculinity is now influencing how African Trinidadians are redefining their own masculinity.

We have based this chapter on a series of individual and focus-group interviews with Indo-Trinidadian men in southern and central Trinidad, first in 2003 and again in 2013, as well as on secondary sources examining some contemporary issues. In both 2003 and 2013, we used the same open-ended questionnaire. We conducted interviews and focus groups with men from different backgrounds, including working-class men of different generations, educated middle-class men, and younger middle-class men (under twenty-five years old) representing the new generation. From these interviews, we can observe a new, creolized notion of masculinity, which in many ways is tied to class position, emerging among young Indo-Trinidadian men.

CREOLE SOCIETY, MASCULINITY, AND GLOBALIZATION

The "Creole Society" model developed by Kamau Brathwaite and discussed in the introduction above provides considerable room for analyzing the changing notions of masculinity in Trinidad and Tobago. During the decolonization process, the African Trinidadian middle class used education as a means of upward mobility and promoted the nationalist cause to gain state power. As described earlier,

European culture was mostly absorbed into the emerging creole culture, which became the dominant hegemonic culture (Reddock 1998). Indo-Trinidadian culture, then, emerged in contestation with African creole culture. In many respects, Indo-Trinidadian culture has remained separate and distinct, although there are instances in which it has been incorporated into, and influenced, the dominant Creole culture. As such, where Indo-Trinidadian culture has become highly incorporated, it competes for cultural space with the dominant national culture. Within the context of globalization, the level of interaction between the Indian and African groups has increased. And while aspects of Indo-Trinidadian culture are absorbed by the dominant creole culture, Indian culture likewise is absorbing elements of creole culture as well as external influences, primarily from Hollywood and Bollywood, to create new hybrid forms of Trinidadian culture. This is particularly evident with the growing popularity of chutney soca (a genre of calypso).

Other than addressing the issue of culture in analyzing masculinity, we also must consider the issue of patriarchy. Patricia Mohammed (1998) argues, as we have noted earlier, that in colonial Trinidad three patriarchies existed in the same geopolitical space: a dominant white patriarchy, a creole patriarchy among African Trinidadians and mixed groups, and an Indo-Trinidadian patriarchy. As creole culture became the dominant culture with decolonization, so, too, did the Creole patriarchy; its rival was the Indo-Trinidadian patriarchy. Creole culture became the centerpiece around which nationalism was constructed to bolster the emergence of the new nation-state. As described in chapter 2, Viranjini Munasinghe (2001, 194) says that, in developing the nation-state in the postindependence period, African creole cultural forms were mobilized to construct national culture. For Indo-Trinidadians, this meant that being nationalistic simultaneously demanded assimilation into African creole culture. In some instances, Indo-Trinidadians assimilated, but at other times they resisted and attempted to make Indo-Trinidadian culture part of the national culture alongside the dominant African creole culture. Analyzing Indo-Trinidadian girlhood within the context of globalization, Gabriella Hosein argues that "it seems more useful to think about these mutually constitutive processes in terms of their divergence, rather than interlock, particularly for this group, rather than for adolescent males" (2012, 3). We want to suggest that, for men, both divergence and intersection are possible.

The discourse on masculinity is located within broader theoretical discussions of gender in particular, and even more broadly within a multilayered system of social stratification. The debate on gender invariably begins with the notion of biological determination. Like racial division, gender stratification results in inequalities. Joan Acker (2004), drawing on the work of Raewyn Connell (2000), argues that the colonial project brought with it large-scale institutions such as armies and bureaucracies, which "'reconstituted' masculinities in the periphery." As such,

> gender was and is inbuilt into the organization of everyday life, but not in the same ways or with the same consequences for everyone. Class and race/ethnic differences, embedded in different histories, mediate the gendered organization of daily life and identity and the gendered deployment of power in the Euro-American capitalist centers and in other countries and areas brought into their orbit through conquest, settlement, colonization, empire and today globalization. (Acker 2004, 24)

Inbuilt into the notion of development and development policy are assumptions about gender that rarely get discussed or analyzed. Some of these ideas about development are predicated on assumptions about the roles of men and women in former colonial societies and mirror similar roles in Europe and North America. Such assumptions are often insensitive to the culture and history of a former colonial society.

The notion of hegemonic masculinity can be used to explain how the process works. Raewyn Connell and James Messerschmidt, commenting on this notion, note:

> Hegemonic masculinity was understood as the pattern of practice (i.e., things done, not just as a set of role expectations or an identity) that allowed men's dominance over women to continue. Hegemonic

masculinities were distinguished from other forms of masculinities, especially subordinate masculinities. Hegemonic masculinity was not assumed to be normal in the statistical sense; only a minority of men might enact it. But it is certainly normative. (2005, 832)

Connell and Messerschmidt go on to point out that "hegemony does not mean violence, although it could be supported by force, it mean[s] ascendency achieved through culture, institutions and persuasion" (2005, 832). They suggest further that "men who receive benefits of the patriarchy without enacting a strong version of masculine dominance could be regarded as showing complicit masculinity" (2005, 832). How men use the tropes of hegemonic masculinity varies. They can adopt hegemonic masculinity when it is desirable to do so, but the same men can then distance themselves strategically from hegemonic masculinity at other times. "Consequently, 'masculinity' represents not only a certain type of man but rather a way that men position themselves through discursive practice" (Connell and Messerschmidt 2005, 841). The notion of hegemonic masculinity, then, is not fixed and universally practiced by all men at all times but rather is fluid and adjustable, at times hidden and at times out in the open.

The process of globalization is not gender neutral. This process has been led largely by men, and hence hegemonic corporate masculinity has been central to its operation. Esther Chow suggests that globalization is a gendered process, and that is ignored by those who assume it is gender neutral. She argues that "much of the theorizing about globalization is either gender-neutral or gender-blind, ignoring how globalization shapes gender relations and people's lives materially, politically, socially and culturally at all levels and treating its differential effects on women and men as similar" (2003, 444). Jean Pyle and Kathryn Ward argue that

> gender has socially constructed components that reflect a society's views regarding appropriate gender roles for men and women and [that] are reinforced by economic, political, social, cultural and religious institutions. Processes of globalization can undermine existing social constructions of gender or cause them to be more firmly

defended. . . . In addition, globalization can combine older and newer forms of appropriate gender roles. (2003, 466)

Acker argues that capitalism separates capitalist production from human reproduction, and, as such, "the division between commodity production in the capitalist economy and reproduction of human beings and their ability to labor has been long identified by feminists as a fundamental process in women's subordination in capitalist societies" (2004, 23). Capitalism has found innovative ways, through outsourcing and the development of sweatshop labor, to generate more profits and perpetuate women's inequality. Acker goes on to argue:

> In today's organizing for globalization, we see the emergence of a hegemonic hyper-masculinity that is aggressive, ruthless, competitive, and adversarial. . . . This masculinity is supported and reinforced by the ethos of the free market, competition, and win-or-die environment. This is the masculine image of those who organize and lead the drive to global control and the opening of markets to international competition. Masculinities embedded in collective practices are part of the context with which certain men make the organizational decisions that drive and shape what is called "globalization" and the "new economy." (2004, 23)

With respect to the construction of masculinity, despite the power of global influences, local factors are also important in understanding of how men behave. According to Linden Lewis, masculinity is

> a whole constellation of practices and behaviors. It is a phenomenon that is not fixed but is always in the process of being negotiated, contested and even destabilized. Masculinity has multiple layers of meaning, which are mediated by acceptance or rejection of societal expectations of behavior, e.g., culture, race, religion, class and sexual orientation. Ultimately, men seek the approval of other men in the performance of their masculinity. They engage in certain gender conventions in an attempt to impose some homogeneity on the category—a homogeneity that is decidedly illusive. (2003, 95)

Lewis's position on masculinity articulates how masculinity is constructed within opposing gender relations on the one hand and within same-gender relations in a racially divided society on the other. Central to this notion of masculinity is the idea of power and control. It is about "acquiring, maintaining or reproducing power, then it invariably comes into conflict with femininity" (Lewis 2003, 97). When this notion is located within the neoliberal model of production, in which race and class are central dimensions of social stratification, the role of gender stereotyping takes on additional meaning. Specifically, masculinity can act as a mechanism to reinforce stereotypes that the broader society holds of specific groups, allowing the perpetuation of domination and hegemony. Within this context, "the ideological process of constructing meaning and identifying one's subject position cannot be formulated without due regard to one's material conditions of existence and to the historical and cultural context of a given society" (Lewis 2003, 98). Given the history of subordination in the Caribbean based on a host of criteria including race, class, gender, and sexuality, the definition and practice of masculinity is determined by one's place in the overall social stratification scheme. Lewis notes that not all European men were part of the hegemonic patriarchal class; however, they derived more benefits from the system than nonhegemonic, non-European males: "In contemporary society, men are engaged in exercising hegemonic power and control over other men of lower classes, different sexual orientations, different races, religions, ethnicities and national origins, inter alia" (2003, 101). Hegemonic masculinity in the Caribbean, then, does not bestow on all men equally access to hegemonic power, and race, class, and local context act as mediating factors.

MASCULINITY IN THE CONTEXT OF THE TRADITIONAL INDO-TRINIDADIAN PATRIARCHY

To understand gender relations within the Indo-Trinidadian community, one has to locate that process within a historical context. Mohammed suggests that the sexual imbalance between men and women during the indenture period, along with the "independent breed" of women who had migrated on their own, set the foundation for gender relations in Trinidad. She argues:

> Indian men could no longer rely on the rules which entrenched patriarchy in India in both the Hindu and Muslim family. On the estate they could not make recourse to the rules governing Hindu life—karma and dharma—which, while glorifying womanhood also placed her in a passive role as a chattel to the male, ensuring her subservience and passivity. They violently coerced their women into submission. (1988, 383)

Over time, however, some elements of this coercive masculinity began to make some concessions; one major concession was in the area of marriage, whereby the man and the woman were now being introduced to each other prior to marriage (Mohammed 1988). Tejaswini Niranjana argues that in their attempt to define their "Indian" identity in the colonial context, Indo-Trinidadians used "Indian nationalist reconstructions of racial and ethnic identities—reconstructions in which definitions of women and what is 'proper' to them occupy a crucial position" (2006, 52). Additionally, Indo-Trinidadian femininity was constructed against the backdrop of African Trinidadian femininity—with emphasis on purity, residence in the private sphere, and submissiveness to the husband.

Gender relations are shaped and reinforced very early on in family structures. Within the traditional Indo-Trinidadian family, a sort of extended family structure was practiced with men at the center. The man was the one who made important decisions for the family. He was expected to be the provider. His masculinity was defined by the fact that he had been provided with a bride whom the elders had agreed upon, particularly his father. He was able to take care of his wife and family, even if that meant living in his parents' home, where his mother would have made the major household decisions. The traditional Indo-Trinidadian man exercised authority over the household, even if that meant at times resorting to violence. Women, conversely, were expected to display subservience. Commenting on the role of a new wife or *doolahin*, Mohammed notes:

> While the "doolaha" or bridegroom could expect to be served by his new "doolahin" in addition to his mother, the new doolahin was expected to shoulder the burden of the household chores, greater acceptance into the new family only coming with the birth of her first child. She was also expected to display evidence of her fertility by producing many sons, another activity which ensured her total domestication and restricted her involvement in any activity in the wider society. (1988, 386)

This situation ensured that the woman's place was in the private sphere while the man's was in the public sphere.

An important indication of Indo-Trinidadian masculinity was the ability of the man to provide for his family. Although in reality many children were born out of wedlock, among the Indo-Trinidadian community this behavior was looked down upon. Children were supposed to be born within wedlock. The role of the man was to father children, and the role of the woman was to take care of the children and remain in the private sphere. Subsequently, young Indo-Trinidadian men were expected, over time, to obtain a piece of land and a house that they could call their own. The accumulation of some degree of personal wealth in the form of one's own residence, regardless of one's social class, was an important indicator of a successful man. Initially, education was viewed with suspicion; however, it soon became an important means of attaining upward social mobility. Carl Campbell (1985) notes that in the 1920s and 1930s a number of "Indian schools" began to emerge. Among middle-class Indo-Trinidadian families, whether Hindu or Presbyterian, educating young men became an important goal.

Another important male responsibility in the traditional Indo-Trinidadian family was ensuring that one's children were married. A man was expected to pass on to his male children the teachings of his culture and the responsibilities associated with manhood.

Traditionally, it was the father's responsibility to find husbands and wives for his children. A premium was placed on having male children over females. In this respect, men were given priority over women for educational investment.

Niels Sampath examined the relationship between creolization, modernity, and masculinity among young Indo-Trinidadian men. He argues that "modernization continues to mean a relative emulation of disciplined Euro-American development while ironically trying to maintain a supposedly 'relaxed' West Indian lifestyle" (1993, 236). In the village Sampath studied, modernization was regarded as the adoption of Western fashions and technology. Those who adopted such trappings were viewed with "suspicion if they acted too bright" (1993, 237). Although the attitudes Sampath observed during his research may have prevailed among rural, working-class Indo-Trinidadian men in the late 1980s, the adoption of Western fashion and tastes is no longer viewed with such suspicion. Instead, those who don't adopt such Western styles are actually viewed as backward and "country-bookie." Sampath correctly notes that Indo-Trinidadian men do attempt to "resist what they may perceive to be the negative aspects of their own 'Indian' identity, and they do so by developing positive/negative self-images, which by contextual definition are ostensibly masculine" (1993, 240). We suggest that those self-images are influenced by class, sexual orientation, and religious concerns. Sampath narrowly views the adoption of creole culture through the process of creolization as "an instrument pertaining to masculine power" (1993, 244). This interpretation of the creolization process assumes that creolization only works from the top down, giving only men the agency to change the patriarchy. Creolization in this context can be seen as "an idiom of adolescent masculinity" (Sampath 1993, 245), but it can also be a more expansive concept.

A combination of the Black Power upheaval (which was a result of the failure of import substitution), the emergence of an activist trade union movement in the 1960s, and the advent of the oil boom in 1972 allowed the state to take a more populist approach to development. It used the revenue from petroleum to become more directly involved in managing the economy—using the new oil revenues to nationalize the petroleum industry, diversify the economy by developing downstream industries from petroleum, build houses and infrastructure, expand education, and create a host of "make-work" schemes aimed at distributing some of the new national wealth to the masses. Greater access to education as well as the expansion of jobs in the state sector provided an avenue for many educated Indo-Trinidadian women to move out of the private sphere and into prominent jobs in the public sphere.

In the 1990s, the wholesale adoption of liberalization and privatization resulted in a shift in the role of government in the economy, radically reforming the civil-service and public-enterprise sectors. This rapid liberalization brought social advancement for some groups and social displacement for others; competition for political power now played out along racial lines. The first Indo-Trinidadian prime minister was elected in 1995, and the first *female* Indo-Trinidadian prime minister was elected in 2010. A female *African* Trinidadian woman has yet to ascend to the heights of political leadership in Trinidad, although women of African descent have served as head of government in Dominica, Jamaica, Haiti, and Bermuda. This situation reflects a contestation for space in the public culture, to control the state and to control resources for redistribution. These developments have also forced changes in gender relations in Trinidad, including notions of masculinity among Indo-Trinidadian men and the way the Indo-Trinidadian patriarchy operates.

INDO-TRINIDADIAN MASCULINITY IN TRANSITION

Indo-Trinidadian men operating within traditional notions of masculinity continue to define their sense of self-worth in the context of a heterosexual family structure. The traditional Indo-Trinidadian family structure includes an extended family, but this structure is evolving. Indian men have customarily thought of masculinity within the context of marriage and family. When asked to identify the essential characteristics of an Indian man, one middle-aged, middle-class, very traditional man replied:

Manhood and masculinity is [sic] really defined by tradition, which heavily involves religion. In the past during the period of indentureship, generally what was considered was arranged marriages. Parents had a very powerful role to play.... The traditional role of male and female in Hindu society has been influenced by the Ramayana, the woman is supposed to be Sita and the ideal man Rama.... What is involved is a heavy responsibility toward making a home work. (interview, July 12, 2003)

A pandit whom we interviewed reacted in a similar manner, saying that being a man involves "getting married [and] being secure in [oneself]. While you are single there are certain things that you can do and nobody questions it, but now that you bring a bride home you have responsibility" (interview, July 6, 2003). The concept of "responsibility" refers to the man's role as provider. Similarly, a working-class father and his son whom we interviewed, and indeed all the young (twenty-five years and younger), upwardly mobile, educated men we talked to, defined their masculinity within the context of a heterosexual family. They all mentioned something about the values that were instilled in them within the family unit.

Across the board, Indo-Trinidadian men see themselves as "taking care of dey family." One of the more religious, older respondents noted that a groom "must be in a position to provide for needs . . . before he marries—so that his wife does not have to go anywhere to get anything" (focus group, August 7, 2013). A younger, working-class married father put it this way: "Well, if ah Indian man have ah family he does wuk hard to see bout he family, that is how I see it—I see my faddah do it. I was small he could not give me everything, but he tried he best, that is how I see it" (interview, August 10, 2013). A retired working-class father illustrated his notion of masculinity as being a provider in the following way:

I might say I did not go to too much school. I leave school when ah was fifteen and ah started to wuk, and then ah had two brothers going to school. The salary I was getting was not much, but you had to make tings do—so I took responsibility to provide for myself as a man. . . .

As for my churren I had to see that they grow up in the proper way, and provide whatever support I could. (interview, August 22, 2003)

Another respondent sought to demonstrate his sense of manhood and responsibility with the following illustration:

> My father died when I was quite young, sixteen years old. My first year of sixth form, I ran the shop and went to school. When I was at university, I ran the shop and went to university. I married my two sisters [meaning arranged their marriages]. . . . I am a teacher, my wife is a teacher, but I sent two girls to law school, and two boys to medical school, and a last daughter to medical school, and I had one who died recently. She had finished a law degree. On two teachers' salary. . . . Along with my wife and my salary I did some farming on the side. (interview, August 10, 2013)

Regardless of their class position, the Indo-Trinidadian men we talked to tended to stress their hard work, readiness to delay gratification, and willingness to sacrifice to attain some material gains that were central to their masculinity. These traits reflected part of the narrative developed by elites in the colonial period that stressed "the importance of savvy, as erudition, as know-how in an unfamiliar and precarious new life" (Khan 2004, 124). Furthermore, the respondents all tended to see their emphasis on hard work and sacrifice as a major difference between themselves and African Trinidadian men.

Whereas most respondents saw providing financially for the family as the major role of the man in the household, they were also slowly beginning to recognize the role of the woman as provider, particularly younger men. Younger men still see the embodiment of masculinity as providing for the family, but in a less uniform way. One respondent, drawing on religion, noted that "men are supposed to be providers and women are supposed to be housewives" (focus group, July 20, 2003). Another noted: "I see myself as being a provider in terms of going out there and achieving goals that you set" (focus group, August 12, 2013). At the same time, however, men are seeing changes that are redefining the provider role. One of the younger respondents noted:

"Traditionally, men were looked upon as providers and the breadwinners in the family. But now that is evolving. Where women are now educating themselves and they are actually competing with men for jobs and they are just as good" (focus group, August 7, 2013). Men's attitude toward women working outside of the home is a fluid one. One respondent noted: "That is the reason why there is so much separation in the world. It is because of the fact that women are becoming more educated so they can provide for themselves and they don't have to depend on any man" (focus group, August 12, 2013). The foregoing comment reveals a bit of apprehension about the changing status of Indian women. It also seems to imply a privileging of the previous social arrangement of Indo-Trinidadian women, over their current mobility. Another respondent, recognizing the changing economic and social realities in Trinidad that require men likewise to adjust their role, reflected: "I would say that his responsibility is still there, expecting to provide, to nurture, and to look after, but at the same time the roles are probably shared. Now women are working and doing the same thing" (focus group, July 20, 2003). The new Indo-Trinidadian men, particularly those who are educated and participate in the globalized world of Hollywood, are beginning to accept that women can have a place in the public arena. The extent and nature of their participation, however, are still a contested terrain.

Some of the men we talked with also defined traditional Indo-Trinidadian masculinity within the context of decision making within the family. One of the older, more traditional men opined: "The woman is the one at home and takes on more of the domestic role even if she may be wuking. The man takes on more of a public role and charts the economic direction of the home" (focus group, August 12, 2013). He went on to illustrate his point:

> I had a very dynamic mother. She would go to Port of Spain and take a bag of rotten potato, separate them, and put them in a bag for sale in the shop. So, if you ask me my mother's influence was very strong, but my father had to protect it. He was very consistent and my mother did not have the consistency or clarity, and she did not oppose my father. She knew he was the leader. At times, she would make decisions, but at times, she would defer to him. (focus group, August 12, 2013)

What seems to be emerging among Indo-Trinidadian men is a recognition of the necessity for women to work outside of the home, but that acknowledgment has not diminished the male role as the head of the household.

Even though Indo-Trinidadian men recognize more and more that women are working outside the home, they still consider household chores the responsibility of women. The working-class men we talked with were willing to entertain the thought of their wives working outside the home, but with limitations. They were prepared to negotiate *some* of the centrality of male authority, up to a point. A retired, working-class father put it this way: "You have to compromise with your wife. . . . I [am] married for forty-two years. . . . We had arguments, but it was never bad. I going to wuk, you is the mudder, and yuh with the churren all day. Yuh have to know what is going on with them. I wont know . . . even if women are educated and they wuk, they should be home by five [PM]" (interview, August 10, 2013). The younger son of this man had a slightly different take on this subject:

> For me, some work is okay. I believe when yuh child come from school you must spend time with them. Ah mean not only the woman but the man, too. I believe the woman could work but be home by the time the churren come home, three–four o'clock in the evening. I also believe that boys should be able to cook, wash, and take care of deyself. If anything happen all yuh could see bout yuhself—but if two people wuking yuh have to help out in the house. (interview, August 10, 2013)

One of the more religious, older male respondents also acknowledged that changes had occurred, but he still reserved certain responsibilities for the father:

> They are supposed to share responsibility together, particularly if they have churren, that is a two-person job. The role of the father is very important in that the mother could only do so much, there comes a time when the mother could do so much but after a certain age some things have to be handed over to the father . . . to teach him man talk. (interview, August 8, 2014)

Clearly, this father is suggesting that the man in the family has a particular duty to teach his sons how to become men.

Whereas traditional Indo-Trinidadian masculinity functions in the public sphere—avoiding connections to the private realm of "woman's work"—as society evolves, men are increasingly redefining their role in complementary ways, rather than in a strictly public/private dichotomized fashion. Among the young, educated Indo-Trinidadian men we talked to, there was more of a sense that women were equal, but whether these men were willing to fully accept women's equality and work alongside them remained ambiguous. They made statements such as: "It is nothing special. You know, man and woman is the same thing." Or: "Like all men, they [women] think they could do anything to a point, and I think that is correct since they should be treated equally." Or: "Generally speaking, I don't see men as superior. I always see women as better than us" (focus group, August 7, 2013). The notion of a househusband was also discussed, and respondents suggested that this idea did not in any way detract from masculinity. Referring to the man as the provider, one respondent noted: "If a man cannot bring stuff into the house, [he] can take the role of the wife and he can provide for the children [meaning child-rearing], like making food, and would still be providing for the family. But that is not the traditional way" (focus group, July 20, 2003). There was some discomfort, however, for some of the men when it came to ceding a share of the provider role to women, since they saw it as a potential source of conflict in the home.

The men we talked to commonly made comparisons between themselves and men of other races. Although many children are born to Indo-Trinidadian men out of wedlock, our respondents nevertheless tended to assign that practice to African Trinidadian men as a behavior not worthy of emulation. A traditional, middle-class man noted: "I would say to my son very early on, 'Do not go around fooling other people's children. What other people do [referring to people of African descent] is their business, but you have a responsibility and you have to set an example for your children'" (interview, July 3, 2003). He reiterated the point as follows:

You cannot father a child and just desert [him or her]. So, there are a number of people whose fathers do not take responsibility for them. In that community [meaning African Trinidadian], they have children all over the place. You would find children of the same age living in different communities having the same father. I know fellas now have three children with different women since they were having relations with many women. The women may need financial support and that is not right, that is not responsible. (interview, July 3, 2003)

One of the young working-class men put it this way: "The Indian man does sacrifice to buy land. That is how he does send he churren to school and university. The Negro man, now he have four woman with outside churren, he renting a house" (focus group, August 7, 2013). A traditional, middle-class man noted: "The creole society [referring to African Trinidadians] have different canons of conduct. The male is a male who does not have fidelity to his mate and his sense of responsibility to his home and to his children" (focus group, August 7, 2013). As with the Indo-Guyanese men examined earlier, many Indo-Trinidadian men have fully embraced this stereotype of their African counterparts. Perhaps using stereotypes is one way these men can distinguish themselves from African Trinidadians, but it definitely signals a sense of moral superiority, irrespective of their own participation in the same reproachable behavior. Even younger, upwardly mobile men tended to blame African Trinidadians for out-of-wedlock children, in an indirect way: "Any man can be a father. It does not take much to impregnate a woman.... In a lot of single-parent homes the children, when they realize [they] could overpower their mother—they would do whatever they want, whereas if the father was there he is seen as one who can lead the family" (focus group, July 20, 2003). In this comment, the limitations on women's authority are evident; note the use of the word "overpower." In contrast, the father is presumed to be the family's legitimate authority and disciplinarian; hence, households lacking men are considered deficient. The young man quoted above was implying that young African Trinidadian men growing up in households without their fathers lack a male authority figure to keep them in line, and so they are prone to lax discipline themselves. Increasingly, Indo-Trinidadians are blaming the lack of fathers or father figures in household for the surge in gang-related crime in the country as well.

One of the older, traditional men saw differences between Indians and Africans with respect to values—specifically implying that African Trinidadians did not value hard work or achievement. Drawing on something he'd read by Lloyd Best, a well-known Trinidadian public intellectual, he noted: "Best made the point when he was comparing the *doubles* vendor [mainly of Indo-Trinidadian descent] and the public servant, and he was looking at the success of the *doubles* people. The others celebrate wine, women, and song. You need to maximize your enjoyment, you can't get enough" (interview, July 15, 2003). A young, working-class respondent articulated his view this way:

> Look, pay was Friday, Monday morning he [an African Trinidadian man] want a dollar from yuh, as soon as he get money he spend, he buy new shoes, the best of threads, ah mean clothes, and food and party. Monday morning, he mopping [begging] a drop [transportation], want something from you to eat and they want a dollar. The Indian man does save he money. Look, I wuking in town [Port of Spain] with some ah dem. Yuh get pay Friday, Monday morning they asking yuh for a cigarette. (interview, July 12, 2003).

A retired working-class father expressed a similar notion:

> There are many Negroes today who say that the Indian man hand kind a tight [thrifty] because they want to save, they want to build a future for dey churren, so if they work for fifty dollars they would spend forty dollars and save the rest. But for the majority of the Negroes they don't want to know where they getting a breakfast from in the morning. . . . When they build a house they say that is "dead money" . . . so they prefer to rent. (interview, August 10, 2013)

The stereotype that African Trinidadian men are not industrious and live a carefree life is still quite strong among Indo-Trinidadian men.

Young, educated, and upwardly mobile Indo-Trinidadian men note the lack of achievement among their African Trinidadian counterparts—in contrast to their own success—but they tend not see the lack of achievement as the consequence of inherent traits but rather due to the circumstances of location. These men emphasized educational achievement as the avenue through which they could achieve a better life and provide for their families, again comparing themselves favorably with their African counterparts: "You tend to find that the Indian men and their families tend to stress more on education whereas African men, they don't see it. It is not so much stressed upon. You would find that the crime and the gangs are committed more by African men simply because of the fact that they tend to neglect education" (focus group, August 12, 2013). Although there was no agreement on the reason for this lack of stress on education as a mechanism for upward mobility, one respondent was instructive:

Everyone wants education for their children. It is who willing to take it, cause like three of us pass for the same school. When we went to school they did not look at creed or race, they look at our marks. They did not know twenty Africans and one hundred Indians or so. They did not look at your name, they looked at your marks, except for the 20 percent from the Ministry [of Education]. So, you could say that the Indian people look to achieve more than Africans, but it not that African parents don't promote education, cause every one want their children to be educated, to learn more and have better things; it is just that those who take it seriously, it is not to say that Africans are not bright people. (focus group, July 20, 2003)

When asked specifically who in the society didn't have any expectations to better themselves, the response was, "the man in the ghetto [referring to the African Trinidadian areas]" (focus group, July 20, 2003).

Among all the respondents, there was serious concern about how the rest of the society interpreted the perceived drive to achieve among Indo-Trinidadian men. This may have been due to the fact that, when we conducted these interviews, there was an Indian-led government in Trinidad mired in allegations of corruption. One of the traditional male respondents noted:

> [Trinidadians in general] have a lot of misconceptions of Indians at large—the question of Indians in government, and how they earn their money and how they get what they have. That is based on sacrifice, with an objective in mind, and it has principles as to how it works. People should not begrudge this, because this what you hearing all over the place. Indians have this and that, but they are not seeing the total sacrifice they are making . . . and the question is, "Are you prepared to do the same thing?" (interview, August 22, 2003).

Similar comments were expressed by a retired, working-class father: "[African Trinidadians] really don't want to know what he did to get that [referring to what Indo-Trinidadian men have achieved], whether he had breakfast, lunch, or dinner when the day come, they don't want to know that, but what they want to know is how he get that in life" (interview, August 12, 2013). A younger working-class man put it this way:

> You see ah Indian man gone to wuk riding he bicycle, carrying he roti and tomatoes, and then in ah few years they see that the man have ah car and ah big house, and they figure he in something [illegal activity]. From the time they see ah Indian man walking barefoot and all of a sudden yuh see he start to build he house, people say he up to something, something about he ent good. (focus group, August 12, 2013)

Among the younger unmarried men, there was some concern about the pressure to sacrifice and achieve the material things that are celebrated by many Indo-Trinidadian men. One respondent expressed the concern in this manner:

> You have to look at the Indian race in particular and see what they have achieved in terms of wealth, business . . . and I seem to notice that they tend to be providers for their family, [but] at times that

affects their family negatively in that they are so caught up in making it that they neglect the family themselves in terms of spending time with their wives and children. I am going to make sure they are well fed and so on. They spend more time working. In terms of social life, it takes a back seat. (focus group, July 20, 2003)

Among the younger, upwardly mobile Indo-Trinidadian men, there is great pride in working hard and providing for the family, but there is also an emerging recognition that men have an additional role within the household, that women need not shoulder all household tasks alone.

In all the interviews, Indo-Trinidadian men defined their masculinity within the context of heterosexuality. Homosexuality was seen as abnormal and against the will of God. A religious, middle-class man gave an interesting response to a question about homosexuality:

In Japanese and Indian culture there is a fair amount of homosexuality. . . . If you were abnormal, a hermaphrodite, you had a community. Not much people were abnormal, [and] if you were abnormal you did not act that way [meaning gay]. Hindus are very tolerant people. They prefer to live in a particular way, [but] they don't have the crustiness to sex, say, like the Catholics—there is no concept of sex and sin. Sex is normal but it must be governed by karma. (interview, July 6, 2003)

This respondent was clearly unaffected by notions of political correctness; hence, the archaic notion of the "abnormality" of homosexuality in his comment. The working-class respondents were not as restrained about homosexuality in their statements:

I would say that is ridiculous, that is wrong. They were not made to be together [meaning men with men]. Men weren't made to be married [to each other], neither two women to be married. God did not make a man for Adam, so this thing—I don't know what to say. You know we have one here [meaning in his village]; he feel he is a woman instead of a man. (interview, August 10, 2013).

We should be quick to point out that the insensitivity to homosexuality and the heteronormative orientation of the above comment is not peculiar to Indo-Trinidadian men; it is fairly common among Caribbean men in general. Even the unmarried middle-class men we talked to were in universal consensus that homosexuality was somehow wrong. One of the respondents played into the male fantasy that lesbianism was okay but not homosexuality: "I think it is wrong. In Genesis, it was Adam and Eve not Adam and Steve. God did not design it like that" (focus group, July 20, 2003).

The popular notion that Indo-Trinidadian men have a problem with alcohol consumption and domestic violence did come up as an issue, but only among the unmarried, upwardly mobile men. Many popular chutney songs celebrate the "rum till I die" mentality. These young men were adamant in their position that the rest of society perceives Indian men as drunkards who inflict violence on their wives and children: "They does say the Indian man go drink he punchin [rum] and he kill he family and kill he self . . . but you cannot blame Peter for Paul. Some of them are abusers but not the majority. Their drinking cannot be blamed on all of us" (focus group, July 20, 2003). This respondent may have been voicing the minority position, however, since in the general culture—and in particular among the popular chutney artists such as Ravi B—the consumption of alcohol is celebrated in a frightening manner. About this phenomenon, Linden Lewis observed:

> Men of African descent dominate the calypso in the Caribbean. Though from time to time men of Indian descent also sing calypso, the genre of music known as chutney has become the preferred performative option for Indian men. A different type of boasting is emerging in this arena, though still laced with sexuality, in that male chutney singers tend to consume alcohol in such songs as "Rum Till I Die" (Adesh Samaroo), "Rum Is Meh Lover" (Ravi B), "More Rum for Me" (Mr. Chankar [Neeshan Prabhoo]), and "Bar Man" (Rikki Jai) who manages to combine the notion of sexual prowess and rum drinking in his chutney song. In addition, most of these songs, whether calypso or chutney, operate out of a decidedly heterosexual, hypermasculine culture of braggadocio. (2014, 20–21)

Whereas there is some recognition of the link between rum consumption and domestic violence, the Indo-Trinidadian men in our focus groups on the whole tended to believe that public violence (crime, drug-related violence, and gang activity) was largely perpetrated by African Trinidadian men. One man spoke indirectly about the presumed culprits: "To tell you the truth, [it is] men on drugs" (this language is code for African Trinidadians who deal drugs). Unmarried men took the same position. They did not respect anyone who "promotes violence," referring to African Trinidadian men, who they see as the reason for crime and violence in society. Or, put differently: "The man I least respect would be the man that pulls you down and at the same time he is not trying to make something of himself. . . . He may do things to pull you down like violence and negative things that would impact on society that would pull it down" (focus group, August 12, 2013). However, denouncing and resisting participation in the culture of rum consumption might prove to be an uphill task, since there is significant pressure for men to participate. Chutney artists' celebration of rum consumption is often used to demonstrate the ability of Indo-Trinidadian men to "fete and wine" like their African Trinidadian counterparts in the public arena.

The changes that have occurred in broader Trinidadian society as a result of globalization are forcing adjustments in how Indo-Trinidadian men define their masculinity. Historical factors such as the organization of colonial society, the way nationalism was constructed for the new nation-state, and the importance of race with respect to how political parties were formed provide the foundations for contesting notions of masculinity. In the postindependence period, the creole patriarchy (which over time became equated with African Trinidadian masculinity) was in open contestation with the Indo-Trinidadian patriarchy. They competed with each other in the political arena, the economic arena, and the cultural arena.

How men experience and practice their masculinity, however, is neither static nor uniform. There are class differences in how masculinity is defined, and, because it is socially practiced, change is an ever-looming possibility. Indo-Trinidadian masculinity was first defined in the context of the traditions brought from India, where women were seen as docile and subservient to men, and as caretakers of the home. This view of women's role coincided with the dominant gender values that came from Europe. Indentureship and the challenges of a new space in Trinidad necessitated some changes. In the postindependence period, structural changes in society also elicited new definitions of Indo-Trinidadian masculinity. Perhaps the most consistent and ultimate marker of Indo-Trinidadian masculinity is its inversion of, or opposition to, African Trinidadian masculinity.

A number of structural changes to society in the postindependence period have provided more spaces for Indo-Trinidadian women to move into, in turn altering how Indo-Trinidadian men define their masculinity. First, the rapid expansion of public education at the secondary and tertiary levels has provided Indo-Trinidadian women with the opportunity to become educated and obtain the tools they need to get jobs outside the home. And second, Trinidad's economy has expanded, and the number of new jobs that have been created in the public and private sectors has likewise provided a space for Indo-Trinidadian women to work outside the home. This process has intensified with the increasing diversification of the economy and the entry of Indo-Trinidadian women to the highest levels of all the professions, including politics. Prior to 1995, African Trinidadian men exclusively held the most important political office in the country, that of prime minister. African and Indo-Trinidadian politicians fought many battles along racial lines. In 1995, an Indo-Trinidadian man was elected prime minister for the first time, and in 2010 an Indo-Trinidadian woman occupied the position.

Structural changes have influenced how the traditional Indo-Trinidadian family operates, and in turn these changes have had an impact on how Indo-Trinidadian masculinity is evolving. These changes are happening in different ways and at different speeds, depending on class position, but they are still emerging in relation to African Trinidadian masculinity. Indeed, African Trinidadian masculinity continues to be central to how Indo-Trinidadian masculinity defines itself, and the influence often works both ways.

The centrality of rum drinking to Indo-Trinidadian masculinity, as promoted by chutney artists, is also spilling over into mainstream soca, as evidenced in the 2014 offerings by Machel Montano, "Happiest Man Alive" ("Ah come out to drink meh rum and live meh life, I'm the happiest man alive") and Farmer Nappy (Darryl Henry), "Big People Party" ("Ah wa[nt] big people party, [ha]ve liquor up inside me"). Indo-Trinidadian men continue to view their masculinity within the context of a heterosexual household. Nevertheless, homosexuals and transgendered people of Indian descent live fairly openly in Trinidadian society. Indian men in Trinidad also continue to place primary emphasis on their role as provider, central within the family. However, educated middle-class men are more likely to see their role in the family as shared with the woman, although still not completely equal. Raewyn Connell and James Messerschmidt note that

> men who receive the benefits of patriarchy without enacting a strong version of masculine dominance could be regarded as [participating in] complicit masculinity.... Hegemonic masculinities therefore come into existence in specific circumstances and are open to historical change. More precisely, there could be a struggle for hegemony, and older forms of masculinity might be displaced by new ones. (2005, 832)

The creolization process is redefining how Indo-Trinidadians define their masculinity, but that redefinition is contradictory. Masculinity retains some traditional elements, while simultaneously forging new dimensions of identity. The class position of some Indo-Trinidadian men allows them to distance themselves from traditional notions of masculinity, whereas in other instances embracing the traditional definitions of masculinity ensures continued male dominance in society.

Conclusion

Our focus on the Indian communities of Guyana and Trinidad has allowed us to consider a number of related issues. First is the extent to which the very powerful influences of globalization and modernization affect notions of identity in these two multiracial societies. Second is the resilience of certain cultural practices, as exemplified by the persistence of the Matikor/Dig Dutty marital ritual, however modified to suit contemporary situations in Guyana and Trinidad. This latter point is intriguing to us; scholars tend to downplay the existence of ritual in many parts of the Caribbean, perhaps because they consider the practice to be more shrouded in mysticism than it is viewed as repeated activity with symbolic meanings. And third, we believe that focusing on the Indian community is useful at a time when racial tensions in both Guyana and Trinidad seem to lie just below the surface of the social fabric.

The Matikor/Dig Dutty ritual represents the persistence of a tradition that reinforces the notion of a specific Indo-Guyanese and Indo-Trinidadian identity. The preservation of this identity is important for the solidarity of this racial group, but it also functions to counter any cultural possibility of becoming absorbed by the generalized creole culture of the Caribbean. This cultural insistence is also important in ensuring the full, democratic flourishing of the experience of cultural diversity in the region. We recognize, however, that as Matikor/Dig Dutty perseveres and retains its essence, it is modified at the same time, as explained above.

Similarly, we see Indo-Guyanese and Indo-Trinidadian masculinity as being constructed and reconstructed in light of changing social circumstances, namely the evolving status and new assertiveness of Indian women, facilitated by feminist activism in the region. These developments have taken place against the backdrop of the powerful globalization and modernization processes. These changes have gone hand in hand with successful attacks on the institution of patriarchy regionally and globally, which have forced Indo-Caribbean masculinity along with others to make adjustments. We are not suggesting that patriarchy has been defeated as an institution by any measure, but we affirm that men have been forced to come to terms with the way they relate to women in society; we have highlighted some of the adjustments that Indo-Caribbean men in Guyana and Trinidad have made in response to these developments, while simultaneously focusing on how men of Indian descent in the Caribbean define their masculinity. In this context, also, we examine how Indo-Guyanese and Indo-Trinidadian men have struggled with traditional and contemporary notions of masculinity.

At least initially, observers believed that the process of modernization would erase much of what had been created in the making of these New World societies. However, much historical, social, and intellectual baggage from the colonial era in Guyana and Trinidad has held over, and creole culture has remained influential. Observers also predicted that the process of globalization, given its power and reach, would eventually flatten out differences in society and lead to homogenization, even in countries on the margins of these changes. In fact, the opposite has occurred. Globalization is undoubtedly an economically and socially powerful force, but racial, ethnic, and cultural differences remain influential, and racial and ethnic identity remains an enduring feature of postcolonial society.

On another level, however, our research focus brings us back to the insights of Amartya Sen, who perceptively noted:

> There are two distinct issues here. First, the recognition that identities are robustly plural, and that the importance of one identity need not obliterate the importance of others. Second, a person has to make

choices—explicitly or by implication—about what relative importance to attach, in a particular context, to the divergent loyalties and
priorities that may compete for precedence. (2006, 19)

Sen's observation about identities is germane to our work on the
Indian community in Guyana and Trinidad. As we pointed out
above, these are multiracial societies. One feels the pressure to claim
an identity, usually associated with one's ancestral homeland. But, at
the same time, there is another type of pressure, namely to conform
to the national identity as Guyanese or Trinidadian.

What is at stake here is the question of making a long-term commitment to racial identification while negotiating the process of national
and regional identity formation. We have argued in this text that racial
differences emerged during the period of slavery and were perpetu-
ated throughout the period of indenture. However, in the postcolonial
period, identity formation has been marked by the development of the
political community, along with a growing appreciation of culture and
history, the dawning of the nation and national consciousness, and
all the attendant myths of belonging to the nation. Whereas people of
African descent in Guyana and Trinidad have been able to fall back
on the numerical and cultural predominance of Africans throughout
the Caribbean region, Indo-Guyanese and Indo-Trinidadians realize
that, beyond their respective countries, the only sizeable populations
of people of Indian descent in the region are in Suriname. The other
islands of the Caribbean have much smaller populations of people
of Indian descent. We argue, therefore, that national and regional
identities placed additional burdens on the Indo-Guyanese and Indo-
Trinidadian populations, thus magnifying the tension mentioned by
Sen over the relative importance attached to the divergent loyalties
associated with the robustly plural nature of identity.

The racial tension identified in our work arises when national
identity is perceived to be heavily influenced by a more dominant
culture, in this case, African culture. The strength of the plurality
of identity is severely strained when Indo-Guyanese and Indo-
Trinidadians begin to feel that to assume a national identity is to
lose a bit of their own racial identity. This dilemma is apparent,

for instance, in the game of cricket: Indians in the Caribbean are expected to show loyalty to the West Indies team even while they may feel closer ties with teams from the subcontinent. Interestingly enough, however, the national loyalty of African Guyanese and African Trinidadians is rarely questioned when they acknowledge any African achievement—a testament to the dominance of African culture in both countries and the broader Caribbean. In light of these observations, Sen notes: "The freedom in choosing our identity in the eyes of others can sometimes be extraordinarily limited" (2006, 31). The vexed question, therefore, is how does one legitimately claim an Indian identity while acknowledging a profound allegiance to the Caribbean? Do Guyanese and Trinidadian societies, in which race continues to be politicized, provide sufficient space to permit the true flourishing of identity? Or must one, from time to time, make the hard decision to prioritize one identity over the other?

Another important consideration is the issue of how robustly plural the concept of identity is, as seen through the lens of creolization. Indo-Caribbean people in Guyana and Trinidad, like their African, Portuguese, Syrian, Lebanese, Chinese, and Amerindian counterparts, are forced to come to terms with the very powerful forces of creolization. With the exception of the Amerindians in Guyana, who have an indigenous anchor in the Caribbean, all other groups have been transplanted to the region and therefore have origins elsewhere. Édouard Glissant captures this historical situation succinctly when he notes: "These people were both deported and imported" (2011, 12). He argues further: "This experience of diversity and its long unnoticed works I label creolisation" (2011, 13). Creolization is a form of survival; an adaptation to a new climate, a new landscape, and a new culture in a foreign land. Initially outnumbered by the African enslaved and formerly enslaved population, the Indian communities in Guyana and Trinidad have overcome their demographic deficits and made their presence felt both politically and economically. Beyond the specific racial impact of Indo-Guyanese and Indo-Trinidadians on Caribbean society are the day-to-day interactions, which result in deep sedimentation at the cultural level, as is evident in the influence of Indian culture on music, dress, cuisine, and religion. In the process, all of these specifically Indo-Caribbean influences have themselves become modified in the Caribbean context in language, nomenclature, and practice; such is the complexity of the creolizing process.

As is to be expected, however, creolization is not a conflict-free process. Nigel Bolland (1992) takes up this argument, more implicitly than explicitly. We believe that Bolland's notion of the dialectical view of creolization, which "draws attention in particular to conflicts in social systems as the chief sources of social change," provides some understanding of the tension mentioned earlier among Indo-Guyanese and Indo-Trinidadians, and the broader racial formation in those societies (Bolland 1992, 65). Historically, this tension was manufactured in the process of indenture, in which a deliberate colonial policy of divide and conquer was implemented. Unfortunately, after independence, the new administrations did little to correct this source of tension and conflict. Therefore, the sense of apprehension and mistrust among Indo-Guyanese and Indo-Trinidadians increased rather than diminished.

Building on colonial racial policies in Trinidad and especially in Guyana, political mobilization along racial lines took on a more strident trajectory. Party mobilization not only marked political and ideological differences but embraced racial differences. Certain districts and constituencies began to vote along strict racial lines. Some of our respondents, especially in Guyana, recognized this politicization of racial difference, indicating that, for the most part, people of Indian and African descent live peacefully together until there was an announcement of a general election, and then people retreated to their racial silos. On those occasions, different racial groups jockey to position themselves in line to benefit from political largesse, gain access to state jobs and resources, and earn a sense that "their people" are in control of the reins of power. We should point out that this claim of relative harmony outside the political season has some merit, insofar as in both Guyana and Trinidad there is a noticeable presence of people of mixed African and Indian descent, suggesting that relationships between the two racial groups are not always conflictual. This observation notwithstanding, it is evident that in both countries tension and conflict reside just below the surface. This conflict manifests itself in terms of which racial group is perceived to have greater access to the best high schools, government largesse, important government appointments and contracts, and openings to civil-service and upper-level management jobs. These are normally areas of competition in any society, but in Guyana and Trinidad, despite the powerful influence of the process of creolization, racial difference tends to be an important intervening variable in explaining social reality.

Many tend to see the creolization process as influenced exclusively by racial considerations, but social class can also have a profound impact on how identity formation takes place. Historically, class had an impact on how the Indo-Guyanese and Indo-Trinidadian populations settled on the estates and who got to define, assign property, and negotiate on behalf of the Indian community. Indeed, the *sidhar* (driver) who supervised gangs of twenty to twenty-five indentured immigrants and served as intermediary between the planter and the indentured workers was usually a person who claimed a higher caste position. *Sidhars* were paid a higher wage than regular indentured workers, and many went on to establish "coolie shops" that provided rice, dal, and curry to the immigrant community. These business establishments later grew to include rum shops (Ramsaran 1993). *Sidhars* were the first to set in motion the process of capital accumulation by exploiting others in their racial grouping, leading to class divisions. As the process of globalization developed and access to education improved, further class divisions began to emerge within the Indo-Guyanese and Indo-Trinidadian populations, which also affected the creolization process.

Along with race, class became an important variable influencing the creolization process for both groups in their respective countries. The emergence of a business class and an educated intelligentsia among both Indo-Guyanese and Indo-Trinidadians has had a profound impact on the identity of both groups and has also influenced the contestation for space in the public arena. In both countries, the Indian business class occupies prominent spaces in the society. However, in neither country can the Indian business class be considered an entrepreneurial class in the purely Schumpeterian sense. Rather, it forms more of a "dependent bourgeoisie," relying on the largesse of the state for survival. Competition for state resources has a distinct class dimension within these principle racial groups. In Trinidad, for example, from independence to 1986, a number of prominent Indo-Trinidadian businesspeople supported the ruling People's National Movement (PNM), enjoying economic access to contracts among other benefits, as well as privileged status, in return for their support. The same scenario held under the People's National Congress (PNC) in Guyana. Class differences also emerge as Indo-Guyanese and Indo-Trinidadians become more educated and compete for jobs in the public sector. In Trinidad, the public sector was once seen as the domain of African Trinidadians; however, over time, competition for those jobs increased because of the rising Indo-Trinidadian intelligentsia. As the Indo-Trinidadian business class and educated elite become more powerful, competition over space in the cultural arena and for public resources increases. These trends lead to questions about Trinidadian "authenticity"; in essence, they seek to redefine what constitutes the country's dominant culture and to incorporate aspects of Indo-Trinidadian culture into the mainstream culture. The educated Indo-Trinidadian middle and business classes have long participated in many elements of African Trinidadian creole culture (carnival and calypso). Their participation, however, indicates not only the influence of the dominant creole culture but also the ability of Indo-Trinidadians to change that culture, as expressed in the popularity of chutney and chutney-soca at carnival. As noted by Chalkdust, *dhalpuri* and *doubles*, foods that are grounded in the indenture experience, are nationally consumed by all groups in society. The same can be said of callaloo and *pelau*, which are grounded in the African experience but are also consumed by all. Such contestation for space to display cultural symbols is also played out in competition for advantageous public policy and access to state resources, which are usually controlled by one racial group or the other. Viranjini Munasinghe suggests: "Indo-Trinidadian protest today is motivated less by discrimination and more by the realization that the legitimation of Afro-Trinidadian supremacy in government is open to challenge" (2001, 247). The same can be implied of the Indo-Guyanese community, which controlled the state for an extended period from the early 1990s until 2015. Creolization is a dynamic process that affects the dominant African creole culture as well as the Indo-Trinidadian and Indo-Guyanese culture. It is therefore not a unidirectional but a multidirectional process.

The creolization process in both Trinidad and Guyana also transpires in a gendered manner. Tejaswini Niranjana, writing about the changing notions of Indo-Trinidadian women in general but in particular as they relate to women's sexuality, notes: "The analysis of contemporary Trinidadian discourses of East Indian women's sexuality has to be placed in the framework of a predominantly biracial society of the island. Indian traditions (and Indian women) in Trinidad come to be defined as those who are not, cannot be allowed to become, African" (2006, 123). A case can also be made that some Indo-Guyanese and Indo-Trinidadian men are likewise undergoing a process of redefining their understanding of masculinity. In both countries, men occupy positions of dominance over women in society. The system of patriarchy that prevails in both countries was carried from India in the overall context of religion. As the process of globalization has continued to spread throughout the region, these respective patriarchies have been challenged, more profoundly in Trinidad than in Guyana given the higher rate of globalization in Trinidad and the extent to which Indo-Trinidadian women are participating in the educational system. Along with these variables, Indo-Guyanese and Indo-Trinidadian masculinity continues to be creolized based on influences that come from outside the Caribbean. Niranjana, reflecting on the criticism that Indo-Trinidadian women face for participating in carnival and chutney-soca, notes: "While the chutney-soca controversy could be read as marking an attempt to re-constitute the Indo-Trinidadian patriarchy, perhaps it could [also] be read as a sign of patriarchy in crisis" (2006, 123). Greater numbers of middle-class Indo-Trinidadian men are themselves adopting influences from outside the Caribbean, in particular from North America, to define their masculinity. Through the creolization process, they are adjusting their notions of masculinity and attempting to redefine the patriarchy. Many Indo-Trinidadian men, particularly those who are young and upwardly mobile, are refusing to equate masculinity with the notion of "rum till I die." What may be emerging is a more creolized Indo-Trinidadian patriarchy that is adopting some elements of African Trinidadian patriarchy along with North American influences.

Creolization, then, is not a linear process that leads to a more homogeneous society but rather a dialectical process that is negotiated along lines of race, class, and gender. Munasinghe argues about Trinidad:

> The renovation of national culture has also brought to the fore the "problem of creolization." There is a tendency among [Hindu] Indo-Trinidadian leaders to anchor Indo-Trinidadian culture in Hinduism. Creolization has been particularly problematic because of the conflation of Hinduism with Indo-Trinidadian culture. Although Creole elements enveloping Indo-Trinidadian cultural forms have the potential of establishing their "nativeness," Indo-Trinidadian and especially Hindu leaders rarely emphasize Creole influences as a justification for national inclusion. Instead, they appeal to their community to abstain from the "wickedness" associated with carnival, bacchanal and fete. (2001, 270)

Contrary to Munasinghe's claim, the fact that Indo-Guyanese and Indo-Trinidadians are expressing their differences does not negate the creolization process. Many see creolization as a movement toward one homogeneous culture that has elements of all previous cultural influences. But creolization as we see it is a dialectical process whereby multiple changing cultures exist side by side, each reformulating elements within their respective contexts. When they compete for control of the state, on the surface, society seems to approximate a model of plurality rather than a creole model. Moreover, the process of creolization is not experienced in the same way by all elements within the respective ethnic groups but is also influenced by class and gender. This ultimately brings us to the much broader question of not just how the Indo-Guyanese and Indo-Trinidadian communities define themselves within their respective societies, but how they define themselves vis-à-vis the broader Caribbean region and how we go about analyzing Indo-Caribbean identity within the broader context of a "Caribbean identity." We put Caribbean identity in quotation marks because this is a contested term but also highly creolized.

The question of identity becomes more salient as the region, driven by the economic factors unleashed by global capitalism, is forced to consider greater integration if it is to survive in the new global order.

Methodological Reflections

It might be useful for those doing research in similar areas, or on similar topics, to consider some of our experiences in the field. We were engaged in data collection for this project in 2003 and again in 2013, in both Guyana and Trinidad. We organized a number of focus groups and in-depth interviews with both Indo-Guyanese and Indo-Trinidadian men and women. We relied mainly on reputational samples, which are commonly used in qualitative research. A number of issues emerged that we had not anticipated. First, in some geographical areas, especially in Guyana, the level of education was very low, and in at least one area this was reflected in the quality of the oral responses. In other areas and with different groups of men, the responses were more thoughtful and in some cases quite substantive. The same was true for Trinidad, where geography and educational attainment sharply influenced the quality of the responses.

Second, while we did in fact anticipate the following eventuality, we were intrigued at the way it manifested itself in the responses of our subjects. We are two Caribbean men of different racial backgrounds. Dave is Indo-Trinidadian and Linden is African Guyanese and Barbadian. When we conducted our interviews as a team, Linden's presence in the research setting influenced the responses of our subjects. Indian men, who were careful to be very polite in the presence of a person of African descent, restrained themselves from actually naming the subject of their criticism. They tended to use the euphemism of "other races of men," or "other people." These were clearly ways of being critical of the African "other" without taking responsibility for any inaccuracy in the accusations leveled at that group of men. Without the African presence on the interviewing team—that is, without Linden present as an interviewer—Indo-Trinidadians, men in particular, felt much more at ease being very critical of African men. The responses of Indo-Trinidadian subjects, interviewed largely by Dave alone, yielded much more pointed criticisms of African Trinidadian men, who, it was suggested, were less morally upstanding, less disciplined, and less responsible than our respondents. In short, the impact of interviewer contamination should not be overlooked in this type of qualitative research. The intricacies of qualitative data collection with respect to race demand in-depth attention especially in the Caribbean, where there is a tendency to borrow wholesale methodological instruments and approaches that are developed outside the region.

Finally, there is much room for additional advanced research among Indo-Guyanese and Indo-Trinidadian men. For example, we investigated Indian masculinity in relation to Hindu men. We restricted our focus because of our interest in Dig Dutty/Matikor, which is a Hindu ritual. It would, however, be interesting to see how religion shapes Indo-Guyanese and Indo-Trinidadian masculinity by interviewing Indians of Muslim and Christian faiths, as well as secular men who practice no religion at all. Lastly, more work needs to be done on the social problem of suicide among people of Indian descent. Guyana has one of the highest suicide rates in the world, and Trinidad also has a very high rate of suicide. It would be useful to investigate these rates by gender and by race. The reasons for the high incidence of suicide in the Indian community are often part of the folklore of racial stereotypes. These suggested areas of research are worthy of further investigation.

Notes

INTRODUCTION

1. Before 1966, this South American country was called British Guiana, to distinguish it from the two other Guianas—Dutch Guiana (now Suriname) and French Guiana, which remains a part of France. At independence, the spelling was changed from Guiana to Guyana. This text uses the postindependence spelling, except within quotations.

CHAPTER 2

1. The Community-Based Environmental Protection and Enhancement Program, or CEPEP, is an agency of the Ministry of Rural Development and Local Government. This special "make-work" scheme was initiated by the government to address the unemployment problem.

2. These areas are inhabited predominantly by poor African Trinidadians.

CHAPTER 3

1. Kali-Mai Puja is a Hindu ceremony in praise of the earth force of Mother Kali, the source of creation and destruction. It is a ceremony of healing and involves the manifestation of spirits and animal sacrifice. The ceremony varies from two days to several days in length.

2. The ritual is called "Dig Dutty" (Dig Dirty) in Guyana, referencing the digging of the earth required by the ritual, while in Trinidad the same ritual is called Matikor.

3. Bhagtas are saints—persons of simplicity and devotion.

4. The Padhatis is a ritual text.

5. We would like to thank Cary Fraser for helping us think through the initial distinction being made here. We would also like to thank Manashi Ray for providing the explanations of the Vedic and Dravidian traditions.

Reference List

Acker, Joan. 2004. "Gender, Capitalism, and Globalization." *Critical Sociology* 30 (1): 17–41.

Allahar, Anton, and Tunku Varadarajan. 1994. "Differential Creolization: East Indians in Trinidad and Guyana." *Indo Caribbean Review* 1 (2): 123–39.

Anderson, Alan. 2001. "The Complexity of Ethnic Identities: A Postmodern Reevaluation." *Identity: An International Journal of Theory and Research* 1 (3): 209–23.

Barlow, Andrew. 2003. *Between Fear and Hope: Globalization and Race in the United States*. Lanham, MD: Rowman and Littlefield.

Bhattacharya, Rahul. 2011. *The Sly Company of People Who Care*. New York: Farrar, Straus and Giroux.

Bolland, Nigel O. 1992. "Creolization and Creole Societies: A Cultural Nationalist View of Caribbean Social History." In *Intellectuals in the Twentieth-Century Caribbean*. Vol. 1, *Spectre of the New Class: The Commonwealth Caribbean*, edited by Alistair Hennessy, 50–79. London: Macmillan Caribbean.

Bonilla-Silva, Eduardo. 2004. "From Bi-Racial to Tri-Racial: Towards a New System of Racial Stratification in the USA." *Ethnic and Racial Studies* 27 (6): 931–50.

Boodhoo, Sarita. 1993. *Kanya Dan: The Ways of Hindu Marriage Rituals*. Port Louis: Mauritius Bhojpuri Institute.

Brathwaite, Kamau. 2005. *The Development of Creole Society in Jamaica, 1770–1820*. Kingston: Ian Randle.

Brereton, Bridget. 1972. "A Social History of Trinidad, 1870–1900." PhD diss., University of the West Indies, Saint Augustine, Trinidad.

———. 1974. "The Foundations of Prejudice: Indians and Africans in Nineteenth-Century Trinidad." *Caribbean Issues* 1 (5): 15–28.

———. 1981. *A History of Modern Trinidad*. London: Heinemann.

——. 1985. "The Experience of Indentureship, 1845–1917." In *Calcutta to Caroni: The East Indians of Trinidad*, edited by John Gaffar La Guerre, 21–32. Saint Augustine, Trinidad: Extra-Mural Studies Unit, University of the West Indies.

Camejo, Acton. 1971. "Racial Discrimination in Employment in the Private Sector in Trinidad and Tobago: A Study of the Business Elite and Social Structure." *Social and Economic Studies* 20 (3): 294–318.

Campbell, Carl. 1972. "Immigration into a Divided Society: A Note on Social Relationships in Trinidad, 1846–1870." Paper presented at the Fourth Annual Conference of Caribbean Historians, University of the West Indies, Kingston.

——. 1985. "The East Indian Revolt against Missionary Education." In *Calcutta To Caroni: The East Indians of Trinidad*, edited by John Gaffar La Guerre, 117–34. Saint Augustine, Trinidad: Extra-Mural Studies Unit, University of the West Indies.

Carter, Martin. 2000. "On Governor and Governed." *Kyk-Over-Al*, nos. 49–50 (June): 79–98.

Chase-Dunn, Christopher. 1999. *Global Formations: Structures of the World Economy*. Cambridge: Blackwell.

Chevannes, Barry. 2001. *Learning to Be a Man: Culture, Socialization, and Gender Identity in Five Caribbean Communities*. Kingston: University of the West Indies Press.

Chow, Esther Ngan-ling. 2003. "Gender Matters: Studying Globalization and Social Change in the 21st Century." *International Sociology* 18 (3): 443–60.

Connell, Raewyn. 2000. *The Men and the Boys*. Berkeley: University of California Press.

——. 2008. "A Thousand Miles from Kind: Men, Masculinities, and Modern Institutions." *Journal of Men's Studies* 16 (3): 237–52.

Connell, Raewyn, and James W. Messerschmidt. 2005. "Hegemonic Masculinity: Rethinking the Concept." *Gender and Society* 19 (6): 829–59.

Craig, Susan. 1982. "Sociological Theorizing in the English-Speaking Caribbean: A Review." In *Contemporary Caribbean: A Sociological Reader*, vol. 2, edited by Susan Craig. Saint Joseph, Trinidad: College Press.

De Barros, Juanita. 2014. *Reproducing the Caribbean: Sex, Gender, and Population Politics after Slavery*. Chapel Hill: University of North Carolina Press.

Douglas, Mary. 2002. *Purity and Danger: An Analysis of Concepts of Pollution and Taboo*. London: Routledge.

Durkheim, Émile. 1995. *The Elementary Forms of Religious Life*. New York: Free Press. First published in 1912 as *Les formes élémentaires de la vie religieuse*.

Farrell, Terrence. 2012a. "No Sacred Cows." *Trinidad Express*, July 16.

——. 2012b. *The Underachieving Society: Development and Policy in Trinidad and Tobago*. Kingston: University of the West Indies Press.

Giddens, Anthony. 2000. *Runaway World: How Globalization Is Reshaping Our Lives*. New York: Routledge.

Glissant, Édouard. 2011. "Creolisation and the Americas." *Caribbean Quarterly* 57 (1): 11–20.

Hall, Stuart. 1996. "Race: The Floating Signifier." Lecture delivered at Goldsmiths, University of London. Video, directed by Sut Jhally. Northampton, MA: Media Education Foundation.

Haraksingh, Kusha. 1999. "Indenture and Self-Emancipation." In *Enterprise of the Indies*, edited by George Lamming, 38–42. Tunapuna, Trinidad: Trinidad and Tobago Institute of the West Indies.

Heath, Roy. 1996. *The Shadow Bride*. New York: Persea Books.

Higman, Barry W. 1978. "African and Creole Slave Patterns in Trinidad." *Journal of Family History* 3 (2): 163–80.

———. 2011. *A Concise History of the Caribbean*. Cambridge: Cambridge University Press.

Hosein, Jamela Gabriella. 2012. "Modern Navigations: Indo-Trinidadian Girlhood and Gender-Differential Creolization." *Caribbean Review of Gender Studies*, no. 6: 1–24.

Hosein, Jamela Gabriella, and Lisa Outar. 2012. "Indo-Caribbean Feminisms: Charting Crossings in Geography, Discourse and Politics." *Caribbean Review of Gender Studies*, no. 6: 1–10.

Kanhai, Roseanne, ed. 1999. *Matikor: The Politics of Identity for Indo-Caribbean Women*. Saint Augustine, Trinidad: School of Continuing Studies, University of the West Indies.

Karran, Kampta. 2000. "The Guyana Kali Mai Puja: A Worship's Metamorphosis." In *Race and Ethnicity in Guyana: Introductory Readings*, edited by Kampta Karran, 183–93. Georgetown, Guyana: Offerings Publications.

Keister, Lisa. 2000. *Wealth in America: Trends in Wealth Inequality*. Cambridge: Cambridge University Press.

Kempadoo, Kamala. 1999. "Negotiating Cultures: A 'Dogla' Perspective." In *Matikor: The Politics of Identity for Indo-Caribbean Women*, edited by Rosanne Kanhai, 103–13. Saint Augustine, Trinidad: School of Continuing Studies, University of the West Indies.

Kerbo, Harold. 2003. *Social Stratification and Inequality: Class Conflict in Historical, Comparative, and Global Perspective*. 5th ed. Boston: McGraw-Hill.

Khan, Aisha. 2004. *Callaloo Nation: Metaphors of Race and Religious Identity among South Asians in Trinidad*. Kingston: University of the West Indies Press.

Klass, Morton. 1961. *East Indians in Trinidad: A Study of Cultural Persistence*. New York: Columbia University Press.

Ladoo, Harold Sonny. 1974. *Yesterdays*. Toronto: House of Anansi Press.

Lamming, George. 1973. "The West Indian People." In *Caribbean Essays: An Anthology*, edited by Andrew Salkey, 5–16. London: Evans Brothers.

———. 2009. *Sovereignty of the Imagination: Conversations III*. Philipsburg, Saint Martin: House of Nehesi Publishers.

Lawrence, Keith O. 1985. "Indians as Permanent Settlers in Trinidad before 1900."
In *Calcutta to Caroni: The East Indians of Trinidad*, edited by John Gaffar La
Guerre, 95–116. Saint Augustine, Trinidad: Extra-Mural Studies Unit, University
of the West Indies.

Lerner, Gerda. 1986. *The Creation of Patriarchy*. New York: Oxford University Press.

Lewis, Gordon. 1968. *The Growth of the Modern West Indies*. New York: Monthly
Review Press.

Lewis, Linden. 2001a. "The Contestation of Race in Barbadian Society and the
Camouflage of Conservatism." In *New Caribbean Thought: A Reader*, edited
by Brian Meeks and Folke Lindahl, 144–95. Kingston: University of the West
Indies Press.

———. 2001b. "Linden Forbes Burnham (1923–85): Unravelling the Paradox of
Post-Colonial Charismatic Leadership in Guyana." In *Caribbean Charisma:
Reflections on Leadership, Legitimacy and Popular Politics*, edited by Anton
Allahar, 92–120. Kingston: Ian Randle.

———. 2003. "Caribbean Masculinities: Unpacking the Narrative." In *The Culture
of Gender and Sexuality in the Caribbean*, edited by Linden Lewis, 94–125.
Gainesville: University Press of Florida.

———. 2014. "Gender and Performativity: Calypso and the Culture of Masculinity."
Caribbean Review of Gender Studies, no. 8: 15–42.

Lucknauth, Rishma. 2009. "Indo-Caribbean Hindu Wedding." Rishma Lucknauth
(blog), October 21. At https://reshirish.wordpress.com/2009/10/21/
indo-caribbean-hindu-wedding/.

Magolda, Peter M. 2003. "Saying Good-Bye: An Anthropological Examination of a
Commencement Ritual." *Journal of College Student Development* 44 (6): 779–96.

Magru, Basdeo. 2005. *The Elusive El Dorado: Essays on the Indian Experience in
Guyana*. Lanham, MD: University Press of America.

Mahabir, Kumar. 2009. "Race Retention and Culture Loss: South Asians/East Indians
in St. Vincent." In *Indian Diaspora in the Caribbean*, edited by Kumar Mahabir,
79–92. New Delhi: Serials Publications.

Manfredi, John. 1982. *The Social Limits of Art*. Amherst: University of Massachusetts
Press.

McNeal, Keith. 2011. *Trance and Modernity in the Southern Caribbean: African
and Hindu Popular Religions in Trinidad and Tobago*. Gainesville: University
Press of Florida.

Mehta, Brinda. 2004. "Kali, Gangamai, and Dougla Consciousness in Moses
Nagamootoo's *Hendree's Cure*." *Callaloo* 27 (2): 542–60.

Melucci, Alberto. 1989. *Nomads of the Present: Social Movements and Individual
Needs in Contemporary Society*. London: Hutchinson Radius.

Mohammed, Patricia. 1988. "The Creolization of Indian Women in Trinidad." In
The Independence Experience, 1962–1987, edited by Selwyn Ryan, 381–98. Saint

Augustine, Trinidad: Institute of Social and Economic Research, University of the West Indies.

———. 1998. "Ram and Sita: The Reconstruction of Gender Identities in Trinidad through Mythology." In *Caribbean Portraits: Essays on Gender Ideologies and Identities*, edited by Christine Barrow, 391–413. Kingston: Ian Randle.

———. 2002. *Gender Negotiation among East Indians in Trinidad, 1917–1947*. New York: Palgrave Macmillan.

Munasinghe, Viranjini. 2001. *Callaloo or Tossed Salad? East Indians and the Cultural Politics of Identity in Trinidad*. Ithaca, NY: Cornell University Press.

Naipaul, V. S. 1989. *A Turn in the South*. New York: Alfred A. Knopf.

———. 2003. *Literary Occasions: Essays*. New York: Alfred A. Knopf.

Nair, Supriya. 2008. "Toxic Domesticity: Home, Family and Indo-Caribbean Women." In *BIM: Arts for the 21st Century* 1 (2): 62–75.

Niranjana, Tejaswini. 2006. *Mobilizing India: Women, Music, and Migration between India and Trinidad*. Durham, NC: Duke University Press.

———. 2011. "Indian Nationalism and Female Sexuality: A Trinidadian Tale." In *Sex and the Citizen: Interrogating the Caribbean*, edited by Faith Smith, 101–24. Charlottesville: University of Virginia Press.

Persaud, Walter. 2005. "Gender, Race and Global Modernity: A Perspective from Thailand." *Globalizations* 2 (1): 210–27.

Pintchman, Tracy. 2004. "Courting Krishna on the Banks of the Ganges: Gender and Power in a Hindu Women's Ritual Tradition." *Comparative Studies of South Asia, Africa and the Middle East* 24 (1): 22–33.

Prashad, Vijay. 2000. *The Karma of Brown Folk*. Minneapolis: University of Minnesota Press.

———. 2012. *Uncle Swami: South Asians in America Today*. New York: New Press.

Premdas, Ralph, and Harold Sitahal. 1991. "Religion and Culture: The Case of Presbyterians in Trinidad's Stratified Society." In *Social and Occupational Stratification in Contemporary Trinidad and Tobago*, edited by Selwyn Ryan, 331–49. Saint Augustine, Trinidad: Institute of Social and Economic Research, University of the West Indies.

Pyle, Jean L., and Kathryn B. Ward. 2003. "Recasting Our Understanding of Gender and Work during Global Restructuring." *International Sociology* 18 (3): 461–89.

Raghunandan, Kavyta. 2012. "Hyphenated Identities: Negotiating 'Indianness' and Being Indo-Trinidadian." *Caribbean Review of Gender Studies*, no. 6: 1–19.

Ramesar, Mariam. 1974. *The Impact of Important Racial Minorities on Colonial Caribbean Society: The East Indians of Trinidad, 1891–1921*. Saint Augustine, Trinidad: Institute of Social and Economic Research, University of the West Indies.

———. 1994. *The Impact of Important Racial Minorities on Colonial Caribbean Society: East Indians of Trinidad, 1891–1922*. Saint Augustine, Trinidad: Institute of Social and Economic Research, University of the West Indies.

Ramsaran, Dave. 1993. *Breaking the Bonds of Indentureship: Indo-Trinidadians in Business.* Saint Augustine, Trinidad: Institute of Social and Economic Research, University of the West Indies.

Ramsaran, Dave, and Derek Price. 2003. "Globalization: A Critical Framework for Understanding Contemporary Social Processes." *Globalization* 3 (2): 23–43.

Reddock, Rhoda. 1998. "Contestation over National Culture in Trinidad and Tobago: Considerations of Ethnicity, Class and Gender." In *Caribbean Portraits: Essays on Gender Ideologies and Identities,* edited by Christine Barrow, 414–35. Kingston: Ian Randle.

Ritzer, George. 2004. *The Globalization of Nothing.* Thousand Oaks, CA: Pine Forge Press.

Rodney, Walter. 1981. *A History of the Guyanese Working People, 1881–1905.* Baltimore: Johns Hopkins University Press.

Roopnarine, Lomarsh. 2017. "Phagwah or Holi: My Favourite Festival." *Guyana Times,* March 7. At http://guyanatimesgy.com/phagwah-or-holi-my-favourite-festival/.

Ryan, Selwyn. 1972. *Race and Nationalism in Trinidad and Tobago.* Toronto: University of Toronto Press.

———. 1991. "Social Stratification in Trinidad and Tobago: Lloyd Braithwaite Revisited." In *Social and Occupational Stratification in Contemporary Trinidad and Tobago,* edited by Selwyn Ryan, 57–79. Saint Augustine, Trinidad: Institute of Social and Economic Research, University of the West Indies.

———. 2013. *No Time to Quit: Engaging Youth at Risk; Executive Report of the Committee on Young Males and Crime in Trinidad and Tobago.* Saint Augustine, Trinidad: Multimedia Productions, School of Education, University of the West Indies.

Sampath, Niels M. 1993. "An Evaluation of the 'Creolization' of Trinidad East Indian Adolescent Masculinity." In *Trinidad Ethnicity,* edited by Kevin Yelvington, 234–53. Knoxville: University of Tennessee Press.

Scarano, Francisco. 1989. "Labor and Society in the Nineteenth Century." In *The Modern Caribbean,* edited by Franklin W. Knight and Colin A. Palmer, 51–84. Chapel Hill: University of North Carolina Press.

Schein, Edgar H. 1992. *Organizational Culture and Leadership.* 2nd ed. San Francisco: John Wiley and Sons.

Seecharan, Clem. 2011. *Mother India's Shadow over El Dorado: Indo-Guyanese Politics and Identity, 1890s–1930s.* Kingston: Ian Randle.

Segal, Daniel. 1993. "Race and Color in Pre-Independence Trinidad and Tobago." In *Trinidad Ethnicity,* edited by Kevin Yelvington, 81–115. Knoxville: University of Tennessee Press.

Seligman, Adam, Robert P. Weller, Michael J. Puett, and Bennett Simon. 2008. *Ritual and Its Consequences: An Essay on the Limits of Sincerity.* Oxford: Oxford University Press.

Sen, Amartya. 2006. *Identity and Violence: The Illusion of Destiny*. New York: Penguin.

Sharma, Nitasha Tamar. 2010. *Hip Hop Desis: South Asian Americans, Blackness, and a Global Race Consciousness*. Durham, NC: Duke University Press.

Shewcharan, Narmala. 1994. *Tomorrow Is Another Day*. Leeds: Peepal Tree Press.

Sivanandan, Ambalavaner. 2005. "Race and Class: The Future." *Race and Class* 46 (3): 1–5.

Smith, Anthony D. 1991. *National Identity*. London: Penguin.

Smith, Michael G. 1960. "Social and Cultural Pluralism." In *Social and Cultural Pluralism in the Caribbean*, edited by Vera Rubin, 763–77. New York: Annals of New York Academy of Sciences.

———. 1965. *The Plural Society in the British West Indies*. Berkeley: University of California Press.

Smith, Raymond T. 1962. *British Guiana*. New York: Oxford University Press.

———. 1964. *British Guiana*. London: Oxford University Press.

Smith, Raymond T., and Chandra Jayawardena. 1958. "Hindu Marriage Customs in British Guiana." *Social and Economic Studies* 7 (2): 176–94.

Spivak, Gayatri. 1999. *A Critique of Postcolonial Reason: Toward a History of the Vanishing Present*. Cambridge, MA: Harvard University Press.

Stephanides, Stephanos. 2000. *Translating Kali's Feast: The Goddess in Indo-Caribbean Ritual and Fiction*. Amsterdam: Rodopi.

Stiglitz, Joseph. 2012. *The Price of Inequality: How Today's Divided Society Endangers Our Future*. New York: W. W. Norton.

Swan, Michael. *British Guiana: The Land of Six Peoples*. London: Her Majesty's Stationery Office, 1957.

Trinidad and Tobago Newsday. 2006. "Too Little Too Late." July 6. At www.newsday .co.tt/editorial/print,0,40239.html, accessed July 6, 2006.

Trinidad Express. 2005a. "Time to Take Back Our Town: Port of Spain, Trinidad and Tobago." August 2. Accessed August 2, 2005.

———. 2005b. "Letters: Think Carefully before Bringing Caricom Workers." August 20. At www.trinidadexpress.com/index.pl/print?id=29556730, accessed August 20, 2005.

———. 2005c. "Panday Charges PNM Racism against Caroni." August 20. At www .trinidadexpress.com/index.pl/print?id=29554552, accessed August 20, 2005.

———. 2006. "Charity and Love for Indians in T&T." June 14. At www.trinidadexpress .com/index/pl/print?id=160966478, accessed August 2, 2006.

Trinidad Guardian. 2002. "More T&T Assets Owned by Foreigners." December 5. At www.trinidadguardian.co.tt/busstory2.html, accessed December 5, 2002.

———. 2005. "Kidnapping Boot on the Next Foot." September 25. At www.guardian .co.tt/archives/2005-09-26/ramlogan.html, accessed July 28, 2006.

———. 2006a. "Follow Scotland Yard." June 11. At www.guardian.co.tt/ramlogan
.html, accessed June 11, 2006.

———. 2006b. "Slap in the Face of Christianity." June 13. At www.guardian.co.tt
/archives/2006-06.html, accessed June 13, 2006.

———. 2007. "T&T Future Being Mortgaged." January 26. At www.guardian.co.tt
/letters.html, accessed January 26, 2007.

Tripathi, Smita. 2009. "Kala Panti Coolitude? East Indian Subjectivity in the
Caribbean." In *Indian Diaspora in the Caribbean*, edited by Kumar Mahabir,
158–67. New Delhi: Serials Publications.

Turner, Victor. 1969. *The Ritual Process: Structure and Anti-Structure.* Ithaca, NY:
Cornell University Press.

Van der Veer, Peter, and Steven Vertovec. 1991. "Brahmanism Abroad: On Caribbean
Hinduism as an Ethnic Religion." *Ethnology* 30 (2): 149–68.

Vena, Jules. 1991. "Race and Gender as Factors of Students' Survival to the Fifth
Form in Trinidad and Tobago." In *Social and Occupational Stratification in
Contemporary Trinidad and Tobago*, edited by Selwyn Ryan, 257–87. Saint
Augustine, Trinidad: Institute of Social and Economic Research, University
of the West Indies.

Webber, A. R. F. 1988. *Those That Be in Bondage: A Tale of Indian Indentures and
Sunlit Western Waters.* Wellesley, MA: Calaloux Publications.

Williams, Brackette F. 1991. *Stains on My Name, War in My Veins: Guyana and the
Politics of Cultural Struggle.* Durham, NC: Duke University Press.

Williams, Eric. 1969. *Inward Hunger: The Education of a Prime Minister.* London:
André Deutsch.

Yen, Hope. "Recession Has Left Whites Far Better Off Than Minorities." Associated
Press. July 26 2011. At http://archive.boston.com/news/nation/washington
/articles/2011/07/26/recession_has_left_whites_far_better_off_than_minorities
/, accessed March 19, 2014.

Young, Robert. 1995. *Colonial Desire: Hybridity in Theory, Culture and Race.* London:
Routledge.

FOCUS GROUPS AND INTERVIEWS

Focus group conducted on August 12, 2013, by Dave Ramsaran. Chaguanas, Trinidad.

Focus group conducted on August 7, 2013, by Dave Ramsaran. South Oropouche,
Trinidad.

Focus group conducted in July 2013, with men in Versailles, by Linden Lewis. West
Bank Demerara, Guyana.

Focus group conducted on July 20, 2003, by Dave Ramsaran. Avocat, Trinidad.

Focus group conducted on June 12, 2003, with men of Tain Settlement, by Linden
Lewis and Dave Ramsaran. Port Mourant, Corentyne, Berbice, Guyana.

Focus group conducted on June 12, 2003, with women of Tain Settlement, by Linden Lewis and Dave Ramsaran. Port Mourant, Corentyne, Berbice, Guyana.

Interview conducted on August 10, 2013, with a father and son, by Dave Ramsaran. South Oropouche, Trinidad.

Interview conducted on August 8, 2013, with a middle-class male, by Dave Ramsaran. San Fernando, Trinidad.

Interview conducted on July 15, 2003, with a secondary school teacher, by Dave Ramsaran. San Fernando, Trinidad.

Interview conducted on August 22, 2003, with a retired working-class male, by Dave Ramsaran. South Oropouche, Trinidad.

Interview conducted on July 12, 2003, with a father and son, by Dave Ramsaran. South Oropouche, Trinidad.

Interview conducted on July 6, 2003, with a pandit, by Dave Ramsaran. Chaguanas, Trinidad.

Interview conducted on July 3, 2003, with a working-class male, by Dave Ramsaran. South Oropouche, Trinidad.

Interview conducted on June 14, 2003, with Pandit Persaud and Sarita Boodhoo, by Linden Lewis and Dave Ramsaran. Kitty, Georgetown, Guyana.

Interview conducted on June 12, 2003, with Rishee Thakur, by Dave Ramsaran and Linden Lewis. Port Mourant, Corentyne, Berbice, Guyana.

Interview conducted on June 10, 2003, with Indrani Sharma, by Linden Lewis and Dave Ramsaran. Georgetown, Guyana.

Interview conducted on June 20, 2002, with Pandit Maharaj, by Dave Ramsaran and Linden Lewis. South Oropouche, Trinidad.

Interview conducted on June 19, 2002, with Ravi Ji, by Dave Ramsaran and Linden Lewis. Chaguanas, Trinidad.

Interview conducted on June 17, 2002, with Lakan Birju, by Dave Ramsaran and Linden Lewis. South Oropouche, Trinidad.

Interview conducted on June 16, 2002, with Ruby Ragoonan, by Dave Ramsaran and Linden Lewis. South Oropouche, Trinidad.

Index

CPSIA information can be obtained
at www.ICGtesting.com
Printed in the USA
BVHW030012090520
578449BV00003B/9

9 781496 828255